SHEPHERDSTOWN
★ IN THE ★
CIVIL WAR

KEVIN R. PAWLAK

SHEPHERDSTOWN ★ IN THE ★ CIVIL WAR

ONE VAST CONFEDERATE HOSPITAL

THE History PRESS

Published by The History Press
Charleston, SC 29403
www.historypress.net

First published 2015

Manufactured in the United States

ISBN 978.1.62619.925.5

Library of Congress Control Number: 2015942272

Dedicated to Private First Class Clifford James Williams,
Thirty-ninth Infantry Regiment, Ninth Infantry Division, killed in action near St. Lo, France, July 24, 1944.
Boston Strong

CONTENTS

Foreword, by James A. Rosebrock	9
Acknowledgements	11
Introduction: “One Vast Hospital”	13
1. “We Labor Under Many Disadvantages”	15
2. “All Is Terrible Suspense”	27
3. The Woe of the Wounded	35
4. “We Surrender! We Are Wounded Men!”	39
5. Shepherdstown, Hospital Town	49
6. “The Longest, Saddest Day”	67
7. “Like an Awful Dream”	91
8. “I Shudder Even Now, in Recalling It”	109
9. “Their Deeds Are Not Forgotten”	127
Notes	135
Bibliography	157
Index	167
About the Author	171

FOREWORD

As the sun slipped toward the western horizon at the end of America's bloodiest day, the cries of thousands of wounded and dying men replaced the roar of cannons and rattle of musket fire in the fields and woodlots around Sharpsburg, Maryland. The casualties were on a scale so appalling that we can barely comprehend it today. There was no hope for the almost four thousand already dead. Thousands of their comrades, who began this day in the ranks of infantry regiments and artillery batteries, now lay wounded upon this field. Their fate was in the hands of the surgeons and their assistants in both armies. The wounded of Antietam were just the latest casualties of the Maryland Campaign. Since the fighting at Solomon's Gap on September 13 through the South Mountain fighting the next day to Jackson's final attack on Harpers Ferry on the fifteenth, the citizens of Shepherdstown had witnessed, ministered to and endured the specter of wounded and dying Confederate soldiers seeking refuge in their town. What had been a trickle became a flash flood of misery on September 17.

All too often, we are inclined to overlook the terrible aftermaths of Civil War battlefields and look forward to the next campaign. More than 150 years have sufficiently distanced and desensitized us to the sights and sounds and smells of those battlefields so that we have little concept of what those places and times were like. There has been less commentary and analysis of the medical history of the war overall perhaps than many other aspects and even less about that of the Confederate side. Much of the reason for the lack of attention to the Confederate medical service is the frustrating scarcity of original material. To an even greater degree, we frequently pass by completely the civilians who stood in the path of the armies and who remained long after their passage, cleaning up the refuse of war and trying to find a new normal.

Kevin Pawlak makes his debut on the literary stage of Civil War history by filling in some of these empty spaces. He is uniquely qualified to take on this important work. As the chief guide at Antietam National Battlefield, I have come to know Kevin very well in the past five years. He is a 2014 graduate with honors in history with an emphasis on the Civil War, from Shepherd University. He came to intimately know the town of Shepherdstown during his years as a student there. He takes us back to that town where so many of the Confederate wounded were treated after the battles of the Maryland Campaign. Kevin served as a seasonal park ranger at Harpers Ferry National Historical Park and became the youngest ever National Park Service certified Antietam Battlefield Guide after completing a particularly rigorous testing and presentation program. He now is a full-time education specialist at the Mosby Heritage Area Association. Kevin is well known among the Antietam guide community as a prodigious researcher. He has brought this subject to life by unearthing scores of original documents and rare pictures. By scanning the bibliography and endnotes of this volume, you will see the many primary sources that he used to craft this work. He tells an engaging and compelling story.

I accompanied Kevin on many trips to the National Archives in Washington, the U.S. Army Heritage and Education Center at Carlisle Barracks and (it seems) every bookstore in between as he researched and prepared this book. In many hours of enjoyable conversation and reflection on mostly Civil War topics, I have come to know and respect him as a serious historian. Kevin represents the next generation of Civil War scholars who will advance the scholarship and historiography of that momentous time.

Kevin has skillfully brought to life the untold story of the undermanned and poorly equipped medical department of the Army of Northern Virginia led by Lafayette Guild, with the story of many of those wounded during the battles of the Maryland Campaign and the people who lived along the Potomac River in the town of Shepherdstown, a place that became "one vast hospital."

James A. Rosebrock
Lieutenant Colonel, U.S. Army (Retired)
Chief Guide, Antietam National Battlefield
Sharpsburg, Maryland

ACKNOWLEDGEMENTS

From the time I first set foot in Shepherdstown, West Virginia, in 2009, the amount of tangible history in the town captivated me, as did the town's awareness of its historic sites and stories. One of its most fascinating stories that especially intrigued me during my time attending Shepherd University was the town's experience during the Maryland Campaign of September 1862. Never did I imagine that I would be in a position to write a book about that story. While much has been written about the Federal hospitals and the wounded recuperating in Maryland following the Battle of Antietam, no study has yet examined the Confederate wounded following America's single bloodiest day. I wanted to write this book to tell that story as well as the story of the Confederate medical corps during the campaign and that of Shepherdstown's citizens who became engulfed by the Army of Northern Virginia in September 1862.

Found within this book are chapters discussing the formation of the Confederate medical corps and its actions during the various battles of the Maryland Campaign. This focus is intertwined with the stories of the men the corps aided as well as the story and history of Shepherdstown and its experience during the campaign. For readability purposes, and to provide an easy-flowing story, this is not a book that delves into the strategy of both armies in Maryland. Rather, the stories of those who found themselves in Shepherdstown alongside the town's residents are told. In order to have a better understanding of what Shepherdstown endured and how it came to be a hospital town, examinations of the town's history, the Confederate army and the Confederate medical corps are necessary.

While one name appears as the author of this book, many people helped with its completion. My thanks first extend to The History Press and my editor there, Candice Lawrence. She has been an excellent help during this lengthy process and has made it as easy as possible along the way. Thanks also go to Marianne Davis, whose eye for typos and punctuation mistakes is invaluable.

I would also like to thank John Coski and Randy Klemm from the Museum of the Confederacy for guiding me through the vast holdings of the museum's library. At Shepherd University's Scarborough Library, I want to thank Josh DiSalvo and Christy Toms for tracking down rare books and articles through interlibrary loan. A word of thanks also goes to Vicki Smith at the Historic Shepherdstown Museum and Jim Surkamp for the use of Shepherdstown images from his collection. Lastly, thanks to Tom Clemens, Dan Vermilya, Gordon Damman, George Best, Mike Galloway and Billy Griffith, each of whom provided help along the way. Without the hospitality of Jim Rosebrock, the research trips required to write this book would not have been possible. I am also indebted to him for his wonderful foreword to this book.

My parents, Jerome and Teresa; siblings, Joe, Rion, Gabriella and Heather; and nieces and nephews, Tristan, Leah, Michael and Samantha, all continually encouraged me and surrendered much of their time with me to allow me to pursue this project.

Lastly, to my fiancée, Kristen, who inspired me to write about this topic in the first place, I could not have finished this book without her love, proofreading and support.

INTRODUCTION
"ONE VAST HOSPITAL"

Upon reaching the crest of Douglas Hill on September 20, 1862, the last day of the Maryland Campaign, Samuel Gilpin and his Third Indiana Cavalry comrades met a perfect panorama. Looking to his left, he had a clear view of the fight raging across the Potomac River between the Union Fifth Corps and A.P. Hill's Confederates. To his front, the small community of Shepherdstown, Virginia, lay immediately across the river. "Hospital flags can be seen on every house, church, and barn," wrote Gilpin, causing him to believe Shepherdstown was "one vast Hospital."[1] Indeed, the inundation of perhaps as many as six thousand tired, hungry and wounded Confederate soldiers into a town of slightly more than one thousand residents required the use of every resource this small town had to offer. Shepherdstown was Antietam's largest field hospital.

Despite its enormity and the abounding accounts from this brief episode in the histories of Shepherdstown and the Army of Northern Virginia, this story has often been ignored—thrown aside even by the Federal hospitals situated around Sharpsburg and Frederick, Maryland, an area more popularly known as "one vast hospital."[2] But the medical story of the Army of Northern Virginia is just as intriguing, if not more so, than that of the Army of the Potomac, and the plight of Shepherdstown's residents is just as apparent as those of western Maryland. This story should not be forgotten. The soldiers and civilians who sought and gave aid in Shepherdstown in September 1862 left enough accounts that this story can be pieced together as one that represents the unique bond between armies and civilians caught in the crossfire.

Civil War–era view of Shepherdstown from Douglas Hill. Note the piers of the bridge burned in 1861 sitting in the river. *Library of Congress.*

Shepherdstown's experience in September 1862 was not unique to many American towns during the Civil War. Even Gilpin's claim of the town being "one vast Hospital" can be found multiple times in contemporary accounts throughout the war. While its homes, public buildings and streets served as charnel houses for thousands of scarred Confederate soldiers, Shepherdstown had become the epicenter of one of the war's most crucial campaigns. Both armies jostled for position around the town while Robert E. Lee's Confederates attempted to continue the campaign. With the town caught in the middle of it all, shells landed among its streets and warehouses, and its fields became the last killing ground of the Maryland Campaign. As one of the town's residents summed it up, when war arrived at Shepherdstown's doorstep, "battles had come to mean to us, as they never had before, blood, wounds, and death."[3]

1
"WE LABOR UNDER MANY DISADVANTAGES"

Hundreds of miles from the nearest battlefield, New Yorkers walking along bustling Broadway must have passed under it countless times—a sign with the haunting words "The Dead of Antietam" scrawled on it. Entering the studio of renowned photographer Mathew Brady in October 1862, curious citizens found themselves ascending a staircase to the second-floor exhibit. Once inside the room, "weird copies of carnage" and "pale faces of the dead" met visitors' unsuspecting eyes.[1] Who were these mangled, bloated, sun-beaten corpses in the photographs? They were the tangible embodiment of the struggle that ensued around Sharpsburg, Maryland, on September 17, 1862—America's bloodiest day.

These images remain some of the most well remembered of the entire Civil War. The familiar images of Confederate corpses lying alongside the Hagerstown Pike, in front of the Dunker Church and inside the Bloody Lane continue to be engrained into the American psyche more than 150 years after Alexander Gardner and James Gibson took them. The several dozen Confederates found lifeless in these photographs are some of the most famous (despite their anonymity) Confederates of the war. Antietam's photographic legacy stems from these images that showed the American public miles from the war's bloody fields what war really looked like.

These grisly photographs only demonstrate a slight portion of the Confederate army's losses at Sharpsburg. Thousands more Confederates that Gardner did not record became casualties on September 17 and, perhaps due to the lack of photographic evidence, have remained in the

Confederate dead along the Hagerstown Turnpike on the Antietam battlefield. *Library of Congress.*

shadows of history. Yet while New Yorkers along Broadway symbolically experienced "the terrible reality and earnestness of war," citizens of Sharpsburg, Boonsboro, Hagerstown and Frederick, Maryland, and Staunton, Richmond, Winchester and Shepherdstown, Virginia experienced it physically.[5] Indeed, the latter four places became inundated with the comrades of the dead Confederates captured by Gardner's camera. Until now, studies of Antietam's victims have focused on Maryland's citizens caught in the path of war, Confederate dead photographed by Gardner and Gibson and the Federal surgeons and wounded in the field hospitals around the battlefield, which also happen to be extensively photographed. However, the story of the Confederate surgeons and the wounded they cared for—as well as that of the citizens of Shepherdstown, who were first in the path of the mass of Confederate wounded—deserves to be told. Like any Civil War story, it cannot be viewed in a vacuum, for the origins of the story of Antietam's Confederate wounded and how they fared during the Maryland Campaign of September 1862 begin in early 1861.

The idea so famously put forth by Confederate general Nathan Bedford Forrest that "war means fighting, and fighting means killing" would not have had much traction in either North or South in April 1861, as both sides expected a short and relatively bloodless conflict.[6] This expectation is reflected in no better way than by examining the readiness of the medical departments of each army for war. For the purpose of this work, we will be looking exclusively at the Confederate medical department.

During wartime, the primary function of a medical department is "keeping the soldier ready for battle and returning him to duty at the earliest

An unidentified surgeon wearing the regulation uniform of a Confederate surgeon. *Library of Congress.*

possible time after illness or injury." Historian Horace H. Cunningham notes that both sides were "ill-prepared" to perform this task at the war's outset.[7] The lack of preparation can be partially traced to legislation authorizing the Confederate medical department, which allotted space for only eleven medical officers in the Confederate army and a mere $350,000 for its functions.[8] Twenty-three former U.S. Army surgeons constituted the burgeoning medical department, a number clearly too small to accommodate the growing Southern army.[9] Size, however, was not the only factor dooming Confederate medical success early. Disorganization, inept medical officers, disease and the small amount of funding led one historian to call the Confederacy's medical corps "anything but encouraging" by July 1861, the month when the medical department faced its first test.[10]

Sunday, July 21, 1861, witnessed the first serious bloodshed of the Civil War. In a battle that was branded as the fight to decide the war, Northerners and Southerners clashed on the plains of Manassas in an all-day battle that left approximately 4,800 Americans killed, wounded or missing. Nearly 1,900 of those fell fighting for the Confederacy. Despite the Confederate victory, disorganization ensued enough to prevent a Confederate counterattack.[11] The performance of the Confederate medical department, however, was valiant but also disorganized. One Confederate wrote, "Our preparations for the battle, so far as the care of the wounded was concerned, were very imperfect."[12] Perhaps sensing this, President Jefferson Davis appointed Samuel Preston Moore to the post of surgeon general on July 30, 1861. Moore's family had an extensive medical background, which, along with his efficiency and previous experience, made him a perfect candidate for the position, which he held for the duration of the war.[13] Shortly following his promotion, Moore set to work preparing the department for a long, protracted war.

Samuel Preston Moore. *From* The Photographic History of the Civil War.

Working from a "single room, crowded to overflowing with employees, soldiers, and visitors on business," Moore began standardizing and professionalizing the Confederate corps of surgeons.[14] He established army medical boards that evaluated the readiness of surgeons for duty (and ousted those who were not), began the construction of numerous hospitals in the South and worked to provide the Confederacy with a reliable source of medical supplies.[15] All of these improvements better prepared the Confederacy's medical corps for the spring campaigns of 1862.

The corps' next call to action in the field came in early April following the Union Army of the Potomac's move to the Yorktown Peninsula, a campaign conducted to capture the Confederate capital, Richmond. However, the medical department's resources were tested not only by battle casualties but also by sickness wrought upon the opposing armies. According to one modern study, conditions were so poor on the Peninsula that, at times, approximately 20 to 30 percent of men in each army could be termed "unfit for duty" due to illness.[16] Despite the sickness, the two armies continued the campaign and met in pitched battle outside Williamsburg, Virginia. This action, fought on May 5, 1862, had important implications for the Confederate medical department.

Casualties in the sharp engagement amounted to less than those at First Manassas—1,682 Confederates and 2,283 Federals.[17] Regardless of the lower numbers, the performance of the Confederate medical corps was worse than it had been ten months earlier. Wounded soldiers were left behind in the Confederate withdrawal, some did not receive any aid and no details were created to remove the wounded from the field in the first place. Two days following the battle, Surgeon General Moore released a circular meant to care "more systematically and effectually for the necessities of the wounded, during and subsequent to engagements." Hospitals at brigade level would be set up in fixed locations beyond the range of enemy fire, each marked by a flag; each hospital and brigade carried all the necessities of nineteenth-century battlefield medical care; and various infirmary corps, consisting of men detailed from the ranks, were responsible for transporting wounded to the rear. In the sense of removing wounded from the battlefield, the importance of Moore's directive cannot be understated. "This order stands as a significant milestone along the bloody way of battle and as one which pointed in the direction of more effective field work," noted one prominent historian.[18]

The new system's first test came several weeks later, ten miles outside Richmond. This time, the bloodletting was the worst yet seen in the war's Eastern Theater. In two days of fighting near a crossroads called Seven

Bringing wounded soldiers to the railroad cars after the Battle of Seven Pines. *Library of Congress.*

Pines, over 11,000 men fell between the two armies (approximately 8,400 of the 11,000 were wounded).[19] When the guns fell silent, the herculean task of caring for the wounded began amid the "groans of the wounded and cries for help."[20] The Confederate medical department performed well in extracting the wounded from the field.[21] Most of the Confederate wounded began to funnel toward the major hospitals in the area, all of which happened to be in the capital of the Confederacy. Richmond's hospitals filled well beyond their capacity, prompting Confederate officers to seize private homes and buildings for hospital purposes. Richmond's streets, homes and warehouses became "one vast hospital."[22] It was not the last time such a grisly term would be applied to a Virginia community.

Even though the Confederacy's stewards, nurses and surgeons were getting closer to perfecting a near impossible art, change soon shook the Confederate army and its medical corps following the fight at Seven Pines. Joseph Johnston, the army's commander, became incapacitated by a wound during the battle and was soon replaced by Robert E. Lee on June 1.[23] Lee quickly brought changes to the medical corps, appointing David C. DeLeon as its chief medical officer.[24] DeLeon's stint only lasted twenty-four days, however. On June 27, 1862, in the middle of one of the war's largest and deadliest campaigns, Lee promoted Alabamian Lafayette Guild to the post of medical director, Army of Northern Virginia.[25] For the next few months, Guild would become acquainted with his new position through a trial by fire.

Born on November 24, 1825, in Tuscaloosa, Alabama, Lafayette Guild grew up around the fields of surgery and medicine—after all, his father was

Prewar image of Lafayette Guild, medical director of the Army of Northern Virginia. *Museum of the Confederacy.*

a doctor. In 1845, Guild graduated from the University of Alabama before attending Jefferson Medical College, which he graduated from in 1848. While Guild attended lectures there, the dean of the school was future Union army commander George B. McClellan's father; Army of the Potomac medical director Jonathan Letterman also graduated from that school. The year following his graduation, Guild joined the U.S. Army. Following service in Florida, Guild served as a surgeon at Governor's Island, New York, where he prevented the spread of yellow fever in the area and thereupon published an influential book about the disease.

In 1851, Lafayette Guild married Aylette Fitts, a native Alabamian. She accompanied Guild on his next assignment, which took him to the American West, where he remained until the beginning of the Civil War. When hostilities erupted, Guild did not renew his oath to the U.S. Army and became one of twenty-three U.S. Army surgeons to join the Confederacy. Guild served various posts throughout the war's early days until becoming the medical director of the Army of Northern Virginia.[26]

Guild's first task came "suddenly and unexpectedly" amid the Seven Days Battles. In a letter written after the campaign, Guild noted the difficulty of his assignment. He had to operate "without instructions of any kind and without knowledge of the previous orders and assignments of medical officers of an army already engaged in action."[27] Yet these deficiencies, Guild believed, did not prevent the medical corps from performing efficiently and effectively, though he did foresee a need for changes that would maximize its potential. More surgeons and better record keeping were two of Guild's legitimate suggestions, though his most serious concern was transportation of the wounded—something Guild called "the old troublesome question."[28]

Likely at the urging of Guild, Lee began to implement changes within his army relating to its medical branch. General Orders No. 94 dealt with one of the largest problems in Lee's army throughout the war: straggling, especially in relation to healthy soldiers leaving the ranks to aid their wounded comrades heading to the rear. Lee ordered that two soldiers from each company be expressly detailed to assist the wounded or bring them to the rear. "No other[s] will be permitted to leave the ranks for this purpose," said the order.[29] This order not only helped quell the problem of straggling in the Army of Northern Virginia but also further defined what the infirmary corps would consist of while also attempting to control the flow of wounded to the rear. Despite improvements such as this, which Guild, in favor of an ambulance corps, did not fully agree with, the lack of surgeons, poor record

Site of Confederate field hospital following the August 9, 1862 Battle of Cedar Mountain. *Library of Congress.*

keeping and the transportation question were far from solved by the time Lee's legions entered Maryland.[30]

Following Lee's neutralization of the Federals on the Peninsula, he began moving his army north to counter yet another Federal force dispatched to seize Richmond. This time, Lee's forces engaged the Federal Army of Virginia at Cedar Mountain on August 9, a sharp fight in the summer heat that forced Guild's corps to deal with not only the wounded but also those crippled by sunstroke.[31] Nearly three weeks later, the two armies met again at nearly the same field where the Confederate medical department's field service began.

The Battle of Second Manassas (August 28–30, 1862) added another nine thousand Confederates to the war's casualty lists and thrust them into Guild's and his surgeons' hands. In contrast to the situation following the fight at Sharpsburg, thousands of Federal wounded were left on the field at Manassas, meaning the Confederates had to care for them, too.[32] Thus, while Lee's army moved toward the Potomac River poised to invade Maryland,

Lee ordered Lafayette Guild to remain behind to remove the Confederate and Federal wounded from the field and parole the approximately three thousand wounded Federals left there.[33]

Removal of the Second Manassas wounded was no easy task, as the surgeon of the Stonewall Brigade noted that Confederate wounded at Manassas were "a good deal scattered."[34] Lee himself feared "there was much suffering among the wounded, but it was impossible to prevent it." The commanding general gave Guild men from each of the army's brigades, as well as "all the means of transportation at our command."[35] It took Guild another week to complete his task; he once again blamed the sluggishness of the process on lack of transportation. Despite Lee's giving Guild as many wagons as the army could spare, it still was not enough. As Guild began to wrap up the Manassas operations and head toward Maryland, he sorrowfully informed Surgeon General Moore, "We labor under *many* disadvantages."[36]

The Federal army also abandoned many of its ambulances in its hasty retreat from the Manassas battlefield. A telling example of the shortage of ambulances in the Army of Northern Virginia and its disorganized state

Scores of Federal ambulances like these were pressed into service by the Confederacy following their capture. *Library of Congress.*

and that of its medical department becomes visible in a dispute over those Federal wagons.

John Bell Hood commanded two infantry brigades in Lee's army; Nathan Evans, who outranked Hood, commanded only one, but in the late stages of the Second Manassas Campaign, the two commands merged into one division. At the end of the battle, Hood's men stumbled upon the coveted prize of abandoned Federal ambulances, which Hood took "with a view to better the outfit of my troops," he wrote. Evans, now senior commander over Hood, ordered the fiery Kentuckian to turn the wagons over to his South Carolinians. Hood refused, believing Evans had no right to them. Hood was subsequently arrested.[37] Thus, the bitter dispute over ambulances—a hot commodity in the Confederate army—placed one of Lee's best fighting generals at the rear of the marching columns as they crossed into Maryland from September 4 to 6.

By September 7, Lafayette Guild had left the task of securing the wounded at Manassas to surgeon James Herndon.[38] Two days later, Guild entered Maryland, ironically, riding in an ambulance—the same manner Robert E. Lee had used to enter the Old Line State three days earlier. Guild later declared the army's ambulances to be "very inferior,"

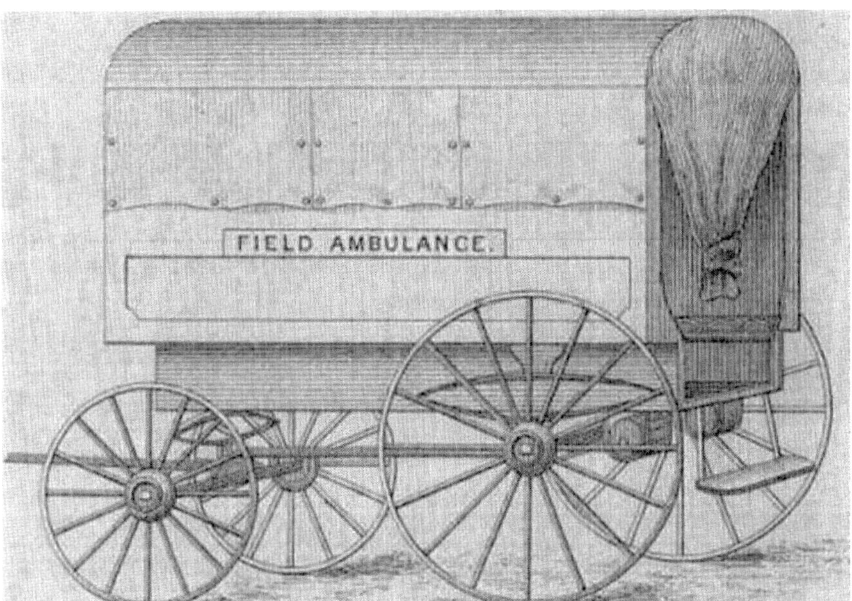

Confederate field ambulance. *From* Atlas to Accompany the Official Records of the Union and Confederate Armies.

a statement no doubt influenced by his ride in one during the Maryland Campaign. Hampered by what he claimed was "a severe disposition," Guild could not mount a horse but vowed to make his way to the army "with as much expedition" as his condition allowed. Little did he know that he was moving toward one of his greatest challenges.[39]

As the Army of Northern Virginia's medical corps moved unknowingly to its test on the banks of Antietam Creek, the corps had improved since the war's early days yet remained imperfect. Field infirmary corps were defined at the brigade and division levels, and the incompetent surgeons had, by this time, been mostly weeded out, thanks to Samuel Moore's army medical boards. However, the South's desire for "final victory obscured the genuine need for further improvement in the field system" and prevented Guild's medical corps from reaching its highest potential.[40]

2

"ALL IS TERRIBLE SUSPENSE"

War was nothing new to Shepherdstown's residents by the summer of 1862. The little town was nestled amid the Shenandoah Valley on the banks of the Potomac River; armies moved back and forth through the area almost as soon as the first shells landed within the walls of Fort Sumter. The town lay "as if forgotten in the bottom of somebody's pocket," wrote one resident. However, war seemed destined to arrive in Shepherdstown. Located "nine miles from everywhere"—a common expression in town—Shepherdstonians found themselves in close proximity to Harpers Ferry, Martinsburg, Williamsport and the Baltimore and Ohio Railroad.[11] Most importantly, the town sat on bluffs directly overlooking the Potomac River, the physical dividing line between North and South. One mile downstream from the town lay a major crossing of that crucial river, known as Boteler's Ford. When the town was first organized, thoughts of a large-scale, domestic war were far from anyone's mind.

The year 1862 marked the 100th anniversary of Shepherdstown's Virginia charter, which made it the oldest town in the land now encompassed within West Virginia.[12] Thomas Shepherd's town grew quickly and, by 1775, was home to nearly one thousand people.[13] Mecklenburg, as Shepherd originally called it, thrived on the power of water, thanks to its location along the Potomac River and a steady stream that meandered through the town aptly called Town Run.[14] It sent companies to fight in the War for Independence, War of 1812 and Mexican War, the latter of which further widened the growing tensions between North and South over the issue of slavery.[15]

Shepherdstown around the time of the Civil War. Trinity Episcopal Church stands at the right of the photograph. *Library of Congress.*

Its location on the northern border of a border state understandably divided Shepherdstown's populace over the troublesome issue. By 1860, 1,178 Shepherdstown residents lived in a county that enslaved 28 percent of its population.[16] Jefferson County, of which Shepherdstown was a part, ranked 68th in percentage of slave population of the 148 counties constituting Virginia in 1860 and the highest of the counties that formed West Virginia in 1863.[17] Despite its seemingly clear leanings toward the Southern lifestyle and numerous accounts of pro-Confederate activities by Shepherdstown's

Above: Postwar view of Boteler's Ford, site of Lee's withdrawal across the Potomac River. *Photographs of Civil War battlefields and cemeteries in Virginia, Maryland and West Virginia. MSS 12529. Special Collections, University of Virginia, Charlottesville, Virginia.*

Right: Reverend Charles Wesley Andrews. *From* Memoir of Reverend C.W. Andrews, D.D.

residents, this was not always the case, although its Southern sympathies were more the rule rather than the exception.

One such exception was Reverend Charles Andrews, a transplanted Vermonter who moved to Shepherdstown in 1842 to become parson of the Trinity Episcopal Church there. Dr. Andrews—another of his illustrious titles—was general agent of the Virginia Colonization Society at one time in his life. Though it was by no means a strictly abolitionist society, Andrews nonetheless used his position within it to free the slaves of his wife and mother-in-law. During his time in Shepherdstown, he supported the African American church there. When hostilities between North and South openly erupted, Andrews opposed the dissolution of the United States, and his Northern and religious convictions prevented him from ever praying explicitly for the Confederate government in church during the war.[18]

Shepherdstown's first taste of interregional conflict came in October 1859, when John Brown and a mixed-race band of men raided the Federal armory and arsenal at Harpers Ferry—a mere dozen miles down the Potomac River from Shepherdstown. Brown and his men hoped to begin a slave insurrection that might end the institution forever in the United States. News of the insurrection brought panic and wild rumors to Shepherdstown. One rumor flowed through town that the insurrectionists were on their way to Shepherdstown following their foray into Harpers Ferry.[19]

In response to the raid, Shepherdstown sent both of its militia companies to help suppress it.[50] Thirty-six hours after the attack began, Brown and his men were either killed, captured or had fled Harpers Ferry. Despite the uprising's brevity, Shepherdstonians, and many in the South, learned from the incident. "The late insurrection at Harper's Ferry should teach the Southern people, in future, to be watchful for the protection of their interests," said a column in the *Shepherdstown Register*. What interests did they seek to protect? Brown's actions and "the very confession of Brown himself behooves the men of the South to be on the alert and prepare means of defence [*sic*] against these infernal abolitionists, whose aim and object is, to liberate the slaves."[51]

Following the raid and in order to further protect their institutions and way of life, Shepherdstown authorized the establishment of a third militia company.[52] As hostilities seemed to be looming, public meetings raised the question of secession should a "Black Republican President" be elected in November 1860.[53] Abraham Lincoln, labeled by the South as a "Black Republican" for his antislavery leanings, was elected. Despite Jefferson County voting against Virginia's secession, it joined the state, and Shepherdstown was thrust into war.[54]

One company of infantry—part of the Stonewall Brigade—and two cavalry companies raised in Shepherdstown fought for the Confederacy.[55] Early in the war, Shepherdstown felt war's cruel hand. In June 1861, Confederates destroyed its only tangible link to Maryland—the covered bridge spanning the Potomac.[56] Then, in December 1861, Federal forces across the river threatened to shell the town if its residents did not cease firing on the Federal pickets. The town council subsequently prohibited the use of firearms in town and attempted to crack down on the sale of liquor. "Our town is filled with widows and children, most of them poor, and the entire population are [*sic*] non-combatants," noted the council. "We solemnly protest in the name of humanity and before the world against vengeance being wreaked upon the innocent, the unprotected, and unoffending."[57] Shepherdstown had averted war for now, but time was running out.

Besides the occasional report of a cannon blast or a skirmish between pickets across the river, 1862 brought more sustained army movements to Shepherdstown and its environs. "We had been 'in the Confederacy' and out of it again," one resident recalled of the summer of 1862. By September 1862, rumors abounded throughout Shepherdstown that the war's two principal Eastern Theater armies were heading in their direction.

Mary Bedinger (right) as a child, along with her mother and brother. *Historic Shepherdstown Museum.*

On September 13, 1862, scores of Confederate stragglers reached Shepherdstown looking for food. Resident Mary "Minnie" Bedinger Mitchell, just twelve years old in 1862, later wrote, "When I say that they were hungry, I convey no impression of the gaunt starvation that looked from their cavernous eyes." Mitchell recollected that the Confederates she saw in September 1862 were the worst soldiers—in terms of their condition—she saw in the whole war. The hungry soldiers

Dr. William Sellman Parran. *Museum of the Confederacy.*

found food and rest in Shepherdstown, before they continued their treks to rejoin their commands or find a new source of subsistence.[58]

Not all of the soldiers who entered Shepherdstown at that time were ravenous and hungry like the stragglers Mitchell remembered. The Parran family of Shepherdstown was one of several families visited by relatives serving in the Confederate army during the Maryland Campaign. Lillie Parran, whose husband, William Fitzhugh Lee—a relative of Robert E. Lee—died as a result of a wound he received on the plains of Manassas on July 21, 1861, found her cousin William Sellman Parran at her doorstep.[59]

The year 1862 marked the culmination of the long and productive career of William Sellman Parran, the latest surgeon in a family filled with such men. Born on June 8, 1834, in Hardy County, now located in West Virginia, Parran attended the Virginia Military Institute; the United States Military Academy; a medical school in Winchester, Virginia; and finally, the University of Maryland, finding varying levels of success at each institution. After completing his studies, Parran settled in Orange County, Virginia; established a medical profession; was married; and had a daughter. The intrepid Parran commanded the local militia unit in Barboursville, Virginia, prior to the war and, upon its commencement, became captain of Company F, Thirteenth Virginia Infantry.[60]

By the summer of 1862, William Parran, now the expectant father of a son, was a surgeon in an artillery battalion in the Army of Northern Virginia.[61] On September 14, Dr. Parran found time to visit his cousin Lillie and Aunt Laura Towner during his trek to Harpers Ferry.[62] The family spoke of bringing William's pregnant wife, Jennie, to Shepherdstown so that she might be closer to her husband and surrounded by his family. "I wish she would do so," William wrote in a letter dated the following day.[63] Whether Jennie ever made it to Shepherdstown is unclear, but in the event that she did, she surely would have found the situation there dramatically different from that which her husband found on September 14.

Similarly, family members serving in the ranks of the Confederate army visited eighteen-year-old Henrietta "Netta" Lee. In her diary, she recorded that two of her cousins serving in the Army of Northern Virginia paid a visit to their family while marching just outside the town on their way to Harpers Ferry. Netta and her friends rode into the countryside to watch the troops march past, not realizing what all of this meant for their town.[64]

The next morning, Sunday, September 14, the citizens of Shepherdstown remained tense, sensing that a large engagement was taking place nearby. Those Shepherdstonians who had enlisted in the Confederate army the previous year and stopped for a few brief moments to visit with their families made it seem that, for a short time, all was right again in the small Virginia community. Suddenly, the roar of distant cannons broke the peaceful stillness, and Shepherdstown was never the same again.

Citizens rushed to their windows and roofs. Peering into the distance, they could faintly make out the smoke rising above the passes of South Mountain

Netta Lee (right) and Pink Boteler. *Historic Shepherdstown Museum.*

and hear the guns booming at Harpers Ferry.[65] "Minnie" Mitchell remembered, "We knew almost nothing except that there was fighting, that it must be very heavy, and that our friends were surely in it somewhere." Finally, as the day continued, most of the citizens could stand the suspense no longer and retreated from their vigils. "It seemed cruel and preposterous to go to bed still ignorant of the result," Mitchell recorded.[66] Soon, Shepherdstown would be well aware of the results, but for now, they had to continue their apprehensive wait. Charles Andrews summed up the feeling perfectly in a letter dated September 17: "All is terrible suspense," he wrote.[67] The worst for Shepherdstown was still to come.

3

THE WOE OF THE WOUNDED

They moved slowly through the pitch-black night, feeling their way along the narrow road to an unknown destination. The long, dark column inched its way forward, gradually moving away from the bloodstained battlefield. Horses neighed, wagons creaked, wounded men groaned, officers shouted orders—the scene "rivaled Bedlam."[68] Finally, after long, grueling hours of stop-and-go marching, a river crossing lit by fires met their eyes. The smoke from the fires blinded the marching soldiers, all while shouted orders, tramping feet and the monotonous rasping of wagon wheels broke the night's silence.[69]

This is the scene of the Confederate withdrawal from Sharpsburg, Maryland, on the night of September 18, 1862. This crossing of the Potomac River stood in stark contrast to the Confederate crossing of it just two weeks earlier. On the heels of another battlefield victory, the Army of Northern Virginia had advanced into Maryland ready to deal the death knell to the United States. They had left the stragglers and wounded behind, and every Confederate who had advanced into the Old Line State seemed ready for another fight.[70] Few of them could have realized, however, how costly the next few fights would be nor how many of them would recross the Potomac River not in a perfect state of jubilation and youth but in a mangled, crippled state in the rear of an ambulance wagon one mile downstream from Shepherdstown.

When examining Robert E. Lee's strategy in the Maryland Campaign, it makes sense that Shepherdstown might fall in the middle of the campaign's

Winchester, Virginia, site of the Army of Northern Virginia's medical and supply depots during the Maryland Campaign. *Library of Congress.*

action. The Army of Northern Virginia crossed into Maryland in early September approximately thirty-five miles downstream from Shepherdstown before it advanced to Frederick, where it rested several days. Then, Lee planned to move west, drawing the Federal army out of Washington City while lengthening its supply lines; at the same time, Lee's supply line through the Shenandoah Valley would become shorter. From there, he could conduct a campaign of maneuver that would exhaust the Federals and give Lee and the Confederacy victory at last.[71]

Lee's first step in the plan involved establishing a forward depot from which he could draw supplies. The intended line, once Lee fully abandoned the old one, stretched from Richmond to Staunton, the two cities connected by the Virginia Central Railroad. From Staunton, supplies moved down the Shenandoah Valley to Winchester.[72] The establishment of Winchester as a forward depot and hospital nearly ensured that Shepherdstown fell within the crosshairs of war, as it did not lie far off the valley's main thoroughfare.

This plan did not solve the supply and transportation problems within the Confederate army, however. Just as Lafayette Guild had said since he took command of the army's medical corps, the transportation problem proved a very large puzzle to solve. This problem did not become any easier to unravel following orders for commanders "to reduce their transportation to a mere sufficiency" prior to entering Maryland, meaning each Confederate regiment entered the Old Line State with one wagon for "hospital, medical stores, &c."[73] Best estimates state that the Army of Northern Virginia brought approximately 2,500 wagons with it into Maryland, a train that would have stretched sixteen miles front to back.[74] In this respect, Lee's forces topped Napoleon's ratio of 12.5 wagons for every thousand men (the Army of Northern Virginia had about 28 wagons for every thousand men in

September 1862).[75] Despite this favorable statistic, Lee continually worried about the lack of transportation for the sick and wounded of his army, and the army's 2,500 wagons consistently proved to be too few in number to accommodate all the army's needs.

On September 3, 1862, Robert E. Lee claimed his army was "feeble in transportation," even though it had recently captured many wagons at Second Manassas.[76] One Maryland citizen noted this as he watched the Confederate army march past. "This rebel army seemed to have been largely supplied with transportation by some United States Quartermaster," he wrote. "Uncle Sam's initials were on many of its wagons, ambulances, and horses. One neat spring-wagon was lettered 'General Casey's Headquarters.'"[77] Even though the Army of Northern Virginia surpassed Napoleon's optimum wagon-to-soldier ratio, it still did not provide enough transportation for the sick and wounded men of the army, meaning that many Confederates wounded in the campaign would have no choice but to walk to safety or be left behind.

One example of the lack of transportation that plagued the Army of Northern Virginia early in the campaign could be found during the Confederate movement west from Frederick, which began on September 10. Prior to the movement, Lee reiterated his order that all sick and crippled soldiers not yet in Maryland proceed to Winchester and the hospitals there.[78] Those sick soldiers and those presently unable to march who made it to Frederick "were to be transported in the ambulances," according to one account.[79] However, for those "who would be injured by the journey," Lee directed that they be left behind in Frederick. Dr. Guild, who by this time had rejoined the army, procured the help of a local physician to care for the estimated forty men the army left in the western Maryland city.[80]

Later correspondence indicates that Lee's army left behind more than forty men. Accordingly, he dispatched Dr. Thomas H. Wingfield, the "medical inspector of field hospitals and camps of the Army of Northern Virginia," to do whatever he could to alleviate this crisis. Lee feared though that the Federals might enter Frederick before the sick could be evacuated.[81] Lee worked to prevent the capture of as many of his sick and wounded as possible throughout the Maryland Campaign, but it was a problem that continued to plague him over the next week and beyond.

Commissary, subsistence and medical stores were also low within the army, and the heads of each department always clamored for more. Luckily for the Army of Northern Virginia, the Federal evacuation of Winchester early in the campaign yielded "a quantity of stores, a large amount of ammunition, some fine guns, medical stores, tents, cooking utensils, &c."[82] Guild's surgeons also found and confiscated medical stores in Frederick—despite the Federals attempting to burn all of theirs before the Confederate arrival—and destroyed what they could not carry.[83] However, the wagons filled with these items often lagged behind the fast-moving infantry, and in the chaos of battle, medical stores could not always be located when they were most desperately needed.[84]

A Georgia soldier described the shortcomings of the Confederate medical department in caring for the sick and wounded in a letter written following the Maryland Campaign: "Our army is very near out of medicines and I have no doubt that many have died for the want of it and proper attention."[85] Perhaps his final words—"proper attention"—reveal that what may have been the greatest deficiency in Guild's medical corps was not a lack of ambulance wagons or medicine; instead, the number of surgeons was well below the number of men requiring medical care. A surgeon in Jackson's command noted following the Battle of Second Manassas that he and an assistant—two men—had to care for about 225 soldiers.[86] The disparity could not have been much different during the Maryland Campaign.

An examination of the Army of Northern Virginia's medical supplies, transportation and number of surgeons at the onset of the campaign in Maryland is revealing. Lafayette Guild and his medical corps clearly had an immense task ahead of them. Despite the deficiencies, though, they had to do the best they could with the limited resources they possessed because it was clear that a severe fight was brewing. Both the Federal and Confederate armies saw this next fight as the one that might determine the war's outcome. Jedediah Hotchkiss, Stonewall Jackson's cartographer, told his wife on September 8, 1862, "Be of good cheer—the skies are brightening for an end to this bloody war. We have to fight once more and we doubt soon."[87] Little did Hotchkiss know how soon the fight would come and how dark the skies would be over western Maryland and Virginia in September 1862.

4
"WE SURRENDER! WE ARE WOUNDED MEN!"

Harpers Ferry/South Mountain Overview

On September 9, 1862, Robert E. Lee issued Special Orders No. 191, a plan that would split his army into several wings with the purpose of reducing the Federal garrisons at Martinsburg and Harpers Ferry, thus securing his supply line through the Shenandoah Valley. The next day, Lee's legions set out from Frederick and by September 13 had surrounded Harpers Ferry. That day, Confederates seized Maryland Heights, the highest prominence overlooking Harpers Ferry. Also on September 13, much of the Union Army of the Potomac entered Frederick, where two soldiers found a misplaced copy of Lee's orders for the campaign. Seizing this opportunity, Union general George B. McClellan devised an ambitious plan to attack the divided Army of Northern Virginia at South Mountain and rescue the Harpers Ferry garrison.

Sunday, September 14, witnessed the Confederate noose around Harpers Ferry tightening as the sounds of battle roared all day on South Mountain. At Turner's Gap to the north, Fox's Gap one mile south and Crampton's Gap farther south, Federal forces attacked the Confederate defenders. Despite Lee's tenacious defense, his positions atop the mountain proved untenable, and he ordered a retreat back into Virginia as well as the abandonment of the Harpers Ferry operation. Upon reaching the heights around Sharpsburg three miles from the Potomac River crossing

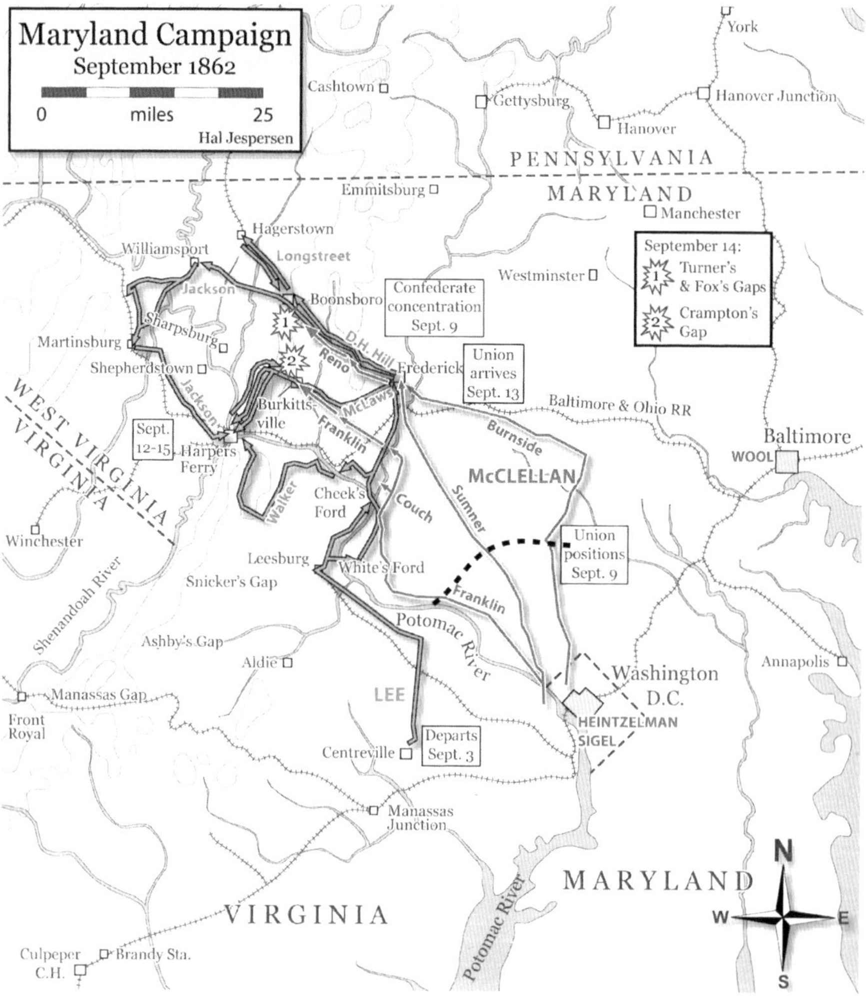

Overview of the Maryland Campaign of September 1862. *Maps by Hal Jespersen, www.cwmaps.com.*

of Boteler's Ford and after hearing of the success of his army at Harpers Ferry, Lee proposed to gather his army at Sharpsburg and continue his campaign. On September 15–16, the opposing armies gathered on the banks of Antietam Creek in preparation for another battle.

Maryland Heights—September 13, 1862

As Colonel D. Wyatt Aiken's South Carolinians slowly inched closer to the Union positions atop Maryland Heights, they found themselves passing through nearly impenetrable terrain. One soldier described it as "almost impassable woods rocks—no road—blind path & no path."[88] In climbing the mountain, the men from the Palmetto State "had to pull themselves up precipitous inclines by the twigs and undergrowth that lined the mountain side, or hold themselves in position by the trees in front."[89]

Before the war, the thirty-four-year-old Aiken had been a professor and newspaper editor from Winnsboro, South Carolina.[90] Now, he found himself involved in seizing the key to Harpers Ferry. Groping its way south toward the Federal defenses, Aiken's command continually stumbled on, harassing Union skirmishers. Finally, after nudging them off again and again, the South Carolinians encountered the main line of defense ensconced behind earthworks "built of great stones and logs, in front of which was an abattis [*sic*] of felled timber and brushwood." Despite the stout appearance of the position, Aiken's men "moved briskly forward, under a heavy fire of musketry," the soldiers having "to cling to bushes while they loaded and fired" due to the uneven terrain.[91] After twenty minutes, they raised a cheer, charged "through the tangled undergrowth, through the abattis [*sic*], and over the breastworks," driving the enemy back.[92]

By the end of September 13, Aiken's South Carolinians helped pry the key to Harpers Ferry from the Federals' hands. However, to Aiken and his men, it came at a ghastly cost: thirteen killed and one hundred wounded in that brief fight.[93] The survivors buried the dead "in the lofty cemetery of Maryland Heights"; for the wounded, as one historian of the battle has succinctly put it, "their ordeal must have been awful," especially due to the scarcity of water atop the mountain.[94] Thus, collecting and caring for the wounded atop Maryland Heights proved to be a trying task for the Confederate medical corps.

Fox's Gap—Morning, September 14, 1862

At 9:00 a.m., musket fire erupted in the woods and fields around Fox's Gap as a brigade of Ohioans struck Samuel Garland's North Carolinians. The battle surged back and forth up the mountainside, and after two hours, neither force could break the stalemate. In an effort to do that, the Federals wheeled two guns to the mountain's summit.[95] Immediately, they began to unleash rounds of canister into the Confederate ranks. To counter the threat, the Twentieth North Carolina's commanding officer dispatched Captain James B. Atwell and his men from Company B to deal with the guns.[96] Atwell, a thirty-year-old farmer from south-central North Carolina, quickly dispatched his men behind a rock outcropping and "picked the gunners off as fast as they could take position around their gun," forcing the abandonment of the pieces by the Federals.[97]

Like a tornado, the fighting at Fox's Gap drew more men into its ferocity. Eventually, John Gorman and his comrades in the Second North Carolina of George B. Anderson's brigade moved south to support the strained North Carolinians already fighting there. Gorman vividly remembered the march to Fox's Gap: "We pass lots of wounded limping down the mountain, trickling blood at every step, then again a stretcher containing some more desperately wounded, and as I bend over one, I catch the pale face of the gallant [Samuel] Garland, who is being carried down desperately wounded in the breast." Garland did not survive his wound despite being rushed off the field by surgeons of the Army of Northern Virginia.[98] Death was at play on South Mountain, and the Confederate medical corps strained to keep up.

Fox's Gap—Evening, September 14, 1862

In the waning daylight, John Bell Hood—no longer under arrest as a result of the ambulance episode at Manassas—and his division moved south to halt the Union breakthrough at Fox's Gap. Despite the growing darkness, the two armies exchanged sporadic gunfire through the still twilight, resulting in a number of casualties, including Federal Ninth Corps commander Jesse Reno. On the opposite end of the field from where Reno fell, the Confederates of Hood's Division also found their comrades falling from this firefight.

Native Alabamian Owen K. McLemore commanded the Fourth Alabama Infantry in Hood's Division. McLemore, a graduate of the United States Military Academy and regular army officer before the war, had already been wounded once in the war at the Battle of Gaines's Mill in June 1862. Recovering, he returned to the Fourth in time for its march into Maryland.[99] Hood called McLemore "a most efficient, gallant, and valuable officer."[100] Unfortunately, as is so often seen in war, gallantry and value do not spare one's life. From his position north of Fox's Gap, McLemore mounted a fence to gain a better understanding of the enemy positions. Soon, a bullet slammed into his shoulder, knocking him from the fence. His Alabamians bore him down the mountain the next morning and conveyed him first to Shepherdstown before moving him to Winchester, where the promising twenty-seven-year-old officer died from his wounds on September 30, 1862.[101]

Turner's Gap—September 14, 1862

Captain John Hoyt, commanding Company K of the Third Alabama, watched from his position on the skirmish line as lines upon lines of Federals formed for their assault and prepared to move toward his vastly outnumbered company. Hoyt must have felt the hopelessness of his mission—to hold back the blue tide as long as possible and prevent them from seizing the summit of South Mountain. That feeling disappeared as his skirmish line erupted in a sheet of flame and smoke.[102] The Federals followed suit, and one ball hit Hoyt, giving him a wound that "badly bruised" his leg. Despite the discomforting wound, he joined an ever-growing procession of wounded moving west from South Mountain, though not without the satisfaction that his men had "made the Yankees 'smell brimstone'" despite the losses they also suffered during the sharp fight. Hoyt proved to be one of the lucky ones, as he returned to the ranks within a matter of weeks following a brief period of recovery in Shepherdstown.[103]

Boonsboro—September 14, 1862

Marching conditions on September 14 were anything but ideal for Civil War armies. Hot, dry and dusty, men consistently fell out of the ranks, especially those Confederates caught up in the march from Hagerstown to the South Mountain battlefield.[104] Surgeons were dispatched behind the marching columns that day "with the duty of picking up the stragglers, and a surgeon is on duty to examine those who 'claim' to be ill," remembered one such member of the medical rear guard, Simon Baruch.[105]

As the marching columns moved closer to the sounds of fighting, many men began to drop from the ranks. "Never before or since have I been

Assistant surgeon Simon Baruch, Third South Carolina Battalion. New York Times.

called upon to examine so many men who complained of being too ill to march or to carry their accoutrements," recalled the surgeon. Despite the terrible marching conditions from the oppressing heat and dust, Baruch attributed the high straggling rate to "emotional influences. When the thunder of distant artillery grows nearer," he said, "cases of this malady begin to appear; they increase in numbers when the sound of musketry rends the air."[106] Another surgeon involved in the march vividly remembered hearing "the booming of cannon in the distance" as aides rushed to bring more troops into the fight.[107] These "emotional influences" and the marching conditions forced many to leave the ranks, leaving Baruch's hands full of stragglers.

Upon finally arriving at the western base of South Mountain after the debilitating march, some soldiers witnessed two ambulances passing by them—one containing the slain Samuel Garland while the other contained the army's commander, Robert E. Lee. With "his arm…in a sling…it would appear that he too is wounded," thought one soldier.[108] Then, the Southerners worked their way up the slopes of the mountain, where they encountered a hectic scene. "Troops of the most demoralized stragglers are descending as we ascend, and long lines of wounded limping down the mountain," noted one Virginian. "The appearances of things are to say the very least discouraging," he continued.[109] Indeed, it was not long before the troops recently rushed from Hagerstown found themselves in a discouraging situation. These Confederates became engaged mostly north of Turner's Gap and were "cut up badly," wrote James Boulware, a surgeon in the Sixth South Carolina Infantry.[110]

Crampton's Gap—September 14, 1862

George Bernard of the Twelfth Virginia Infantry watched as the fence line 250 yards ahead of him became "disclosed by the flashes of light and puffs of white smoke darting out from the muzzles of one, two,

Sergeant George Bernard, Twelfth Virginia Infantry, lies amid Confederate wounded who surrendered to their Northern foes at the base of Crampton's Gap. *From* War Talks of Confederate Veterans.

three, and then it seemed a hundred rifles, the blaze of the guns in a second's time running down the whole length of the enemy's line posted behind the wall."[111] Once the fighting at Crampton's Gap commenced, it erupted into a stand-up, knockout firefight. George Bernard recalled his regiment's response to the Federal onslaught: "Our men at once vigorously returned the fire, which is kept up for nearly an hour." Shortly after the fight's opening, he felt a sensation he had never felt before, as a bullet ripped into his right leg, "as if some heavy substance had struck it with great force." Having stopped the flow of blood, all Bernard could do was lie behind the stone wall in front of him as the balls whizzed around him.[112]

The fighting at the base of the mountain had become so constant and fierce that one Confederate "did not think it was possible…to escape." Perhaps worse for the men on the firing line were the cries of the wounded calling for aid from nearby surgeons. One member of the ambulance corps did manage to miraculously carry a wounded man up the mountain away from the battle by himself.[113] The Union fire was clearly taking its toll on the already thin Southern line. Finally, over an hour after the impasse had begun, the blue line surged forward and broke the back of the Confederate forces pinned in their positions at the base of Crampton's Gap, sending many scurrying up the mountainside.[114]

Not all the gray-clad troops were lucky enough to escape the advancing enemy. George Bernard was not able to join the gray tide retreating up the mountain due to his decrepit and wounded state. Upon the Federals' advance, Bernard attached a handkerchief to his ramrod, waved it above the wall he lay behind and shouted to the Yankees, "We surrender! We are wounded men!" He and several of his comrades were subsequently ushered off to a Federal hospital, where they recovered in the hands of the United States Army.[115]

Those Southern wounded not left behind in the hasty retreat up South Mountain were seen streaming to the rear and descending the west side of the mountain as Confederate reinforcements ascended that same incline.[116] However, not even these extra troops could stem the tide, and the Confederates ceded the crucial Crampton's Gap to McClellan's army.

Pleasant Valley—September 14–15, 1862

Similar to the situation six miles to the north, panic and confusion reigned supreme within Confederate lines in Pleasant Valley, the low land between Elk Ridge to the west and South Mountain to its east. Southwest of Crampton's Gap, Southern leaders vainly tried to rally the remnants of their commands. "Hundreds of soldiers, many of them wounded, were arriving in disorderly array from the fight, while guns and caissons, huddled together with waggons [*sic*] and ambulances, moving towards the rear, blocked up the road," wrote an eyewitness of the scene.[117]

Once in Pleasant Valley, the Crampton's Gap wounded—or, at least, those not captured by the Federals and removed to their hospitals—entered the hospitals in Pleasant Valley, comingling with the wounded from the Maryland Heights fighting a day earlier. Extraction of wounded soldiers from battlefields situated atop mountains like Elk Ridge and South Mountain proved to be particularly trying for the Confederate medical corps. Thomas Salmond and his medical crew of Kershaw's South Carolina brigade had a predominantly difficult time, "as their ambulances and [medical] stores could not be brought upon the mountain [Elk Ridge]."[118] Once the Herculean task of finding and transporting all of the wounded to Pleasant Valley by hand was complete, Salmond and his men could finally treat the wounded in a place where water and supplies were more readily available.

Whether in Pleasant Valley, atop South Mountain or below in Boonsboro, the night of September 14 must have been greatly uncomfortable for the entirety of the Army of Northern Virginia. The long, hot day had sapped the soldiers' energies well before they even entered the fight. Now, that night, they would be asked to conduct a quiet, nighttime withdrawal in the face of the enemy. Where they were going, they could only surmise.

The night must have also been a long one for Lafayette Guild as he began to seek a safe haven for the growing number of Southern wounded. None—from the highest commander to the lowliest private—knew for sure what tomorrow might bring. "Anxious feelings in all our bosoms," one Confederate confided to his diary that night. More work was at hand, however, for Lee, Guild and the thousands of Confederates still in Maryland, as all believed "tomorrow [would] be a bloody day."[119]

5
SHEPHERDSTOWN, HOSPITAL TOWN

Compared to September 14, 1862, when Shepherdstown's residents anxiously watched the smoke and flame of battle obscure South Mountain, September 15 began as a less eventful day. True, Shepherdstonians had to deal with and sort out all of the rumors flowing into town while fearing for the safety of their loved ones whom they knew were involved in the fight, but the unease of watching and hearing a far-off battle was gone. Mary Bedinger Mitchell remembered "sitting about in disconsolate fashion" amid the rumors, when one of the family slaves rushed into the house. In a state of panic and astonishment, the slave proceeded to tell Minnie and her family of a line of wagons crossing one mile downstream from town at Boteler's Ford and moving toward town. Phonetically recording the slave's exasperated comments, Mitchell remembered her saying "dey [the wagons] is full ob wounded men, and de blood runnin' outen dem dat deep," she said as she gauged on her arm how much blood she meant.[120] Shepherdstown's trying time "of strife and carnage" had begun.[121]

Before the wounded of the Army of Northern Virginia descended on the homes, warehouses and churches of Shepherdstown, they had to wind their way off South Mountain, maneuver through the hamlets and fields of western Maryland and across the Potomac River, where they believed safety awaited them. Slowly, the Army of Northern Virginia began to break its contact with its Federal counterpart and begin an agonizingly chaotic and sluggish withdrawal. "We had a bad night on the mountain," began Moxley Sorrel's recollection of the Confederate retreat from South

Modern-day view of the South Mountain battlefields from Shepherdstown (the far mountain range). Boteler's Ford is in the right-center of the picture. *Author's collection.*

Mountain. General James Longstreet's staffer recalled the descent from the mountain passes near Boonsboro: "The mountain roads were filled with broken regiments and companies and it was very late before they got to the foot of the mountain and in some sort of order." "Some sort of order" describes the Army of Northern Virginia's retreat toward the Potomac perfectly, for as one historian has written of this retreat, "considering the circumstances…it went quite well, although there was confusion."[122] Indeed, the past months of hard campaigning, marching and fighting, as well as the recent struggle at the South Mountain passes, had severely fatigued Lee's legions.

A member of the Fourth Alabama remembered that when orders reached them to retreat, "most of the men were asleep, in spite of the efforts of the officers to keep them awake."[123] In at least one instance, the fatigue of the army nearly resulted in several units being left behind.[124] Despite the confusion, the Army of Northern Virginia managed to extract itself from South Mountain without a major calamity befalling it. However, whereas the Confederates kept most of their fighting men in the ranks to fight another day, they also had to abandon many casualties of the September 14 battle in order for Lee to get away from the Federals in a timely manner.

Major G. Moxley Sorrel, assistant adjutant general to James Longstreet. Sorrel was wounded at Antietam and treated in the Hamtramck home on German Street. *From* The Photographic History of the Civil War.

Whether or not Southern units abandoned their wounded from the South Mountain battlefields varied from unit to unit. For example, a member of the Fifth Alabama reported "leaving all our wounded in the enemy's hands."[125] Randolph Abbott Shotwell of the Eighth Virginia left a detailed and horrifying account of leaving the wounded from his unit behind. Shotwell called his wounded comrades "those patient sufferers, who lie among the rocks and bushes awaiting death, or perchance shuddering at the thought of the surgeon's knife, and mournfully listening to the retiring footsteps of their comrades, as they march away amid the gloom. Occasionally the agonized cry of 'water, water! kill me or give me a drink of water!' startled the night air." Rather than retreating from the enemy and leaving his comrades to them, Shotwell determined he would prefer to fight again the next day "than to abandon the field and our wounded to the foe."[126] That, however, was never an option. While some grudgingly left their comrades behind, most Southern units managed to retrieve all of the wounded before leaving their positions atop the mountain.[127]

Despite the inconsistencies as to whether Confederate wounded were transported from the South Mountain battlefield or not by members of their own medical corps, it is clear that a vast majority of the no less than 1,396 wounded Southerners ended up making their way behind their own lines before proceeding to a yet unknown destination beyond the Potomac River. However, for every five Confederates wounded in the battle, four either went missing in action or became Federal prisoners of war. Likely, most of the 1,110 soldiers who fell into the latter category were wounded Confederates captured by the Unionists.[128]

The ground upon which the Confederates defended the South Mountain passes was strewn with the dead and dying and littered with the accoutrements of war. One eyewitness remembered vividly the Confederate positions after the battle. "The ground was strewn with their [Confederates'] dead. Many of the poor fellows had been pierced with two or three bullets. It was a sickening sight to see them lying there just as they had fallen and my heart went out in sympathy for them and the dear ones they left behind."[129] Not all of these Confederates that this United States soldier saw had lost their chance to ever see and talk to their loved ones again. Many of them still clung to life and continued to do so in the hands of their Federal captors.

Due to the hurried and disorganized retreat from their positions at the base of South Mountain and then from its crest, most of the Confederate wounded who fell into Union hands fought in the battle at Crampton's Gap. More than three hundred wounded Confederates came under the care of the Federal surgeons in that area, according to the northern commander there.[130] A wounded Federal wrote that the Confederates received the same care as their Northern counterparts.[131] This fact seems true when comparing mortality rates between Union and Confederate wounded from that battle; 16 percent of the captured Confederates died from their wounds compared to 14 percent of all Union wounded.[132] Southern wounded at the other two passes in the mountain were also removed to the rear of the Union Army of the Potomac where they could be properly taken care of.[133]

The Confederate wounded who were able to escape or be carried off the field faced a much more arduous and grueling journey to safety and aid. So, too, did the Confederate medical corps, which once again became flooded with scores of wounded soldiers. This time however, the situation was very different from anything it had faced before.

First Manassas, the Seven Days' Battles, Second Manassas—all were battlefields that the Confederacy retained control of following the fighting. South Mountain was the first time that Robert E. Lee and his Army of Northern Virginia were forced to leave the field of battle in the enemy's hands. As such, this called for extraordinary measures in order to remove as many wounded as possible from the mountain gaps. Then, once Guild's surgeons completed that difficult task, the next step was to find a suitable—and safe—place for the wounded to be treated.

In an effort to aid Guild and his infirmary corps in the process of finding and hauling off all the wounded, Robert E. Lee assigned a company of Marylanders to "act with the Ambulance train in aiding and bringing the wounded from the field." This impromptu infirmary company fell under the command of John Heard, a citizen of Frederick who, six days earlier, had called upon his fellow Marylanders—the descendants of his state's "Revolutionary glory"—to "achieve the independence of your own State." "Falter not, hesitate not, now that the opportunity is offered you—but rally at once and vindicate your history," he urged any Marylander game enough to join him.[134] Those who followed probably did not envision being assigned to the Army of Northern Virginia's ambulance corps—an assignment that must have very quickly dispelled any hopeful notions of achieving glory on the battlefield. These Marylanders were subjected to the true horrors of war early in their term of enlistment.

Also aiding Lafayette Guild and his surgical corps during the campaign was John Herbig's infirmary corps from Richmond. Early in the war, Herbig called on Jefferson Davis to allow him to form a company "to take charge of the wounded on the battlefield and render them immediate aid and provide the means for their proper conveyance to the hospital ardently." The Confederate government did not approve Herbig's idea until late February 1862, but upon receiving word of its passage, Herbig quickly set to work gathering recruits.[135] In a newspaper advertisement calling for men to join the command, Herbig more succinctly stated the corps' goals. "This company's duties will be to attend the wounded soldiers on a field of battle, and to prevent them from bleeding to death. The company will be stationed a short distance in the rear of the line of battle, to immediately dress the wounds of each soldier wounded and remove him from the field to some proper hospital."[136] Herbig's wagons and surgeons remained in Virginia until the late stages of the Maryland Campaign, when Guild, perhaps realizing the enormity of his task, called on their aid.[137]

Whether Guild had all his resources at hand or not does not take away from the difficulty of finding and securing over one thousand wounded Confederates in the dark of night and bringing them to safe locations where their wounds could be treated. The first place Guild settled on for sending the Army of Northern Virginia's wounded was the town of Boonsboro, which sat at the western base of South Mountain.

The scene amid Boonsboro's log-jammed streets gave citizens and soldiers alike a preview of the scene soon to fall on Shepherdstown only twelve hours from the time the Army of Northern Virginia moved through

Boonsboro in the early morning hours of September 15, 1862. "Hundreds of our wounded are gathered in this little village, crowding the porches and steps of the houses and begging admittance," wrote one of the members of the mass of Confederate soldiers slogging their way through the cramped streets of the town on their way toward the Potomac River. However, unlike the coming scene in Shepherdstown, Boonsboro's citizens were less inclined to aid or shelter the Confederate wounded. Out of fear of attracting trouble from the Federals on the other side of South Mountain should they harbor Confederate soldiers, most of the citizens in the western Maryland town told "these poor victims of war to go away."[138] Indeed, surgeon James Boulware of South Carolina—always one for a colorful description of western Maryland's settlements—called Boonsboro a "Union town of the deepest dye."[139]

Yet it was not only the obvious Union sympathies that compelled Lafayette Guild to seek a better place to establish a hospital of some sort for the South Mountain wounded and those from the army's future movements. Despite the oft-repeated complaint of the Confederate medical department of the Army of Northern Virginia that "the movements of the Army cannot be anticipated…for the General Commanding never discloses any of his plans to those around him," it seemed obvious to Guild that the Confederate presence in Boonsboro was anything but permanent.[140] Thus, several doctors were dispatched by Guild and Lee to remain in Boonsboro with the wounded who were too seriously injured to be moved while the rest of the army moved west toward Shepherdstown and Virginia.

John Mutius Gaines was one such Confederate surgeon. Since the war's outset, Gaines had been using his medical skills to aid those whose blood had been spilt in the North-South conflict. He had been a boarder at the famous Marshall House Hotel in Alexandria, Virginia, when the innkeeper struck down Colonel Elmer Ellsworth after he removed a secessionist flag from the hotel's roof in the early days of the war. The innkeeper was subsequently wounded and Gaines tended to him in his dying hours.[141]

The aforementioned South Carolina surgeon Simon Baruch also received orders to remain in Boonsboro with the seriously wounded Southerners. Having fallen asleep beneath a wagon from the day's exhaustion, Baruch was startled awake in the dead of night by an officer who informed him of his task. When the morning of September 15 dawned, Baruch proceeded to the Disciples Church, where he found seventy-five wounded Confederates sprawled across the sanctuary's floor. "Their wounds had been hastily dressed on the battlefield, but demanded immediate attention," Baruch later recalled.[142]

The South Carolinian quickly set up an impromptu operating table outside the church. There, he pried the door off an abandoned home nearby, placed it on two barrels and began his work. Baruch remembered the scene as he operated on his first South Mountain victim: "The retreating troops were marching past in good order; no firing was heard; indeed no sound but that of rumbling wagon[s] and artillery trains disturbed the air. Intent upon the serious work before me, I was rudely awakened to a realization that 'war is hell.'"[113]

Suddenly, "the rattle of musketry pierced the peaceful air, followed by the clattering of a thousand hoofs and the discomforting spattering of bullets upon the upper walls and roofs of the houses" of Boonsboro.[114] Among the southern cavalry, officers yelled to their troopers, "Mount! Mount!" Boonsboro's streets suddenly became a mass of confused and panicked Confederate horsemen fleeing from the Federal cavalry entering Boonsboro.[115] Baruch, caught in the middle of the maelstrom, safely removed his wounded patient to safety inside the Disciples Church, "and we all breathed freely."[116] The Union horsemen seized upon their surprise charge and scattered the Confederate force. "A general stampede followed," wrote one of the gray-clad troopers, "our whole force rushing from the town" in the direction of Sharpsburg and Shepherdstown.[117] The fight amid Boonsboro's streets "ended as suddenly as it began," and it ended with Union forces occupying the town.[118] Simon Baruch, John Gaines and the scores of Southern wounded hospitalized in Boonsboro found themselves Federal captives.

Caught up in the Confederate retreat was none other than Robert E. Lee's son William Henry Fitzhugh "Rooney" Lee, commander of the Ninth Virginia Cavalry, the unit that had done the lion's share of the street fighting in Boonsboro.[119] On the outskirts of town, a Union bullet killed Rooney Lee's horse, causing him to fall to the ground underneath the weight of the horse. There he lay "dust-covered and bruised" while the fight surged back and forth over him.[150] A Confederate counterattack gave several Southerners enough time to lift the dead horse off Lee's body but not enough time to bring the hurt man back to Southern lines. The dazed Lee remained by the roadside, going wholly unnoticed as the blue columns passed him by. Slowly, the younger Lee inched his way into a stand of trees, where he found a handful of Confederate stragglers. Together, they raised him up, supported his every step and found him a horse. He guided the horse through the western Maryland countryside, crossed Antietam Creek and continued farther to the rear to seek medical aid.[151]

Colonel William Henry Fitzhugh "Rooney" Lee, Ninth Virginia Cavalry. *Library of Congress.*

Rooney Lee went farther than he might have anticipated and found shelter at Ferry Hill Place, the stately plantation home overlooking the Potomac River and, beyond that, Shepherdstown, Virginia. There, the family of Henry Kyd Douglas, the youngest officer on Stonewall Jackson's staff, gave Lee and several other wounded Confederate officers "such ministrations" as they could offer.[152] Meanwhile, one mile downstream from Ferry Hill, scores of bloodstained men with faces grimed in gunpowder and sweat crossed the Potomac River back into Virginia and found the first shelter they could. Shepherdstown lay directly in their path.

Upon preliminary examination, it seems that the Army of Northern Virginia's sick and wounded gravitated toward Shepherdstown simply because it was the first oasis of safety on their route of march. Accounts from Shepherdstown's citizens give the impression that wounded soldiers appeared unexpectedly and unannounced. While this may have been true to a certain extent, it does not seem likely that Confederate wounded wandered over the roads of western Maryland with no direction at all. Due to the lack of pertinent records of this topic, Robert E. Lee's and Lafayette Guild's decisions regarding the army's sick and wounded must be conjectured based on the available evidence.

Due solely to their proximities to the fighting, the primary Confederate field hospitals were initially established on or before September 14, 1862, at Boonsboro for the wounded from the fighting at Turner's and Fox's Gaps; in Pleasant Valley south of Crampton's Gap for the wounded from that battle and the battle for possession of Maryland Heights; and in Charlestown, Virginia, for the wounded from the Harpers Ferry operation.[153] Following the fall of Harpers Ferry on September 15, the Confederates from Pleasant Valley were removed to Charlestown, a place well behind Confederate lines by that point in the campaign.[154]

Once Robert E. Lee decided to retreat from South Mountain and make his way toward Boteler's Ford on the Potomac River, it was obvious that all those wounded who were well enough to be moved had to be evacuated from Boonsboro. Lee's plans changed during the course of the retreat from South Mountain, and he determined to resurrect his campaign in Maryland.

The Southern commander first determined to make a stand at Keedysville, Maryland, approximately three miles west of Boonsboro.[155] The commonly accepted notion within army medical corps of the time stated that larger and more permanent field hospitals, or infirmaries, should be established "in villages, farm houses or barns, without the range of projectiles—but in all cases, so that free communication may be maintained with the front which is in action, and with the rear, whence is to be derived the ambulance wagons and carts to transport the wounded to some fixed hospital in the interior."[156] Likely following these guidelines, it seems logical that Guild would have planned to initially establish such a hospital in Sharpsburg, another three and a half miles to the west, since it was the next town behind Confederate lines out of range of enemy guns.

In the early morning hours, Robert E. Lee made another change of plans and decided to make his stand on the heights just east of Sharpsburg behind Antietam Creek.[157] The exchange of artillery fire across the creek on the afternoon of September 15 must have proved to Guild—if he did not already think it improbable—that Sharpsburg was now too dangerous for it to be a hospital site. Again gazing west from Sharpsburg, Guild found the next significant cluster of buildings to be Shepherdstown.

Shepherdstown was far enough removed behind Confederate lines that it was well out of reach of the Federal long arm but still close enough to

Charlestown, Virginia. Sketch by Alfred Waud. *Library of Congress.*

the front where wounded could be hurriedly transported there. Many warehouses and large churches also filled the town's streetscape. These large public buildings would allow for the hospitalization of a large number of sick and wounded soldiers. In addition to these attributes, Boteler's Ford, though far from a perfect military ford, provided an easy—and refreshing—access between the front lines and the major field hospitals. Lastly, Shepherdstown hardly lacked a significant water supply, thanks to its location on the south shore of the Potomac River. With these factors in its "favor," Shepherdstown became the next—and ultimately last—in a series of temporary sanctuaries for the Confederate wounded of the Maryland Campaign.

One other factor that may have weighed on Guild's mind—although the necessity of having a town such as Shepherdstown so well suited to support the Confederate wounded likely made this point moot—was the intense Southern sympathies expressed within Shepherdstown. As mentioned previously, exceptions to this rule did exist, but accounts of Shepherdstown's citizens denying the admittance of any sick and wounded into their homes, as was the case in Boonsboro, are rare, if they even exist at all. Many Confederate soldiers who passed through the town during this period noted its Southern leanings. "This little village of Shepherdstown is the most intensely Southern place I ever saw," wrote a member of the Richmond Howitzers.[158] Confederate wounded in Shepherdstown had little chance of the town's citizens denying them shelter.

Guild likewise would have seen that beyond Sharpsburg's western boundary sat several prominent farmhouses amid large, open farm fields. These homes could be used as headquarters by the medical staff as well as hospitals for those too seriously hurt to be moved any significant distance

from the battlefield. The fields surrounding the farms would also serve as an ideal location for the army's wagon park, which of course included the army's ambulances. It is certain that the army's ambulances were stationed in the fields west of Sharpsburg on September 17 and probably the days leading up to the battle. The area "all the way between the river and the battle-field was crowded with ordnance wagons and ambulances," especially the road, a gray-clad diarist noted.[159] The proximity of ambulances to the infirmary stations closest to the front lines was essential to removing wounded farther behind the lines, where they could be more effectively treated.

The last factor making Shepherdstown a suitable hospital site for Lafayette Guild was the roads emanating from and entering the town. A direct road led from Sharpsburg to Shepherdstown, and even though the bridge carrying that road across the Potomac had been destroyed in 1861, it remained a reliable route. At the bridge site, boats were impressed into the service of the Confederate States army to bring wounded across the river. Improvements were also made to a farm lane, which branched off the Sharpsburg-Shepherdstown Road, leading directly to Boteler's Ford. W.T. Field of the Fourth South Carolina Battalion remembered after the war that much of his unit was designated "as a pioneer corps to repair the roads to and a ford [Boteler's Ford] on the Potomac River" in order to facilitate the army's movements should it have to withdraw but also to ease the trek of the wounded.[160]

Upon Lee's decision to stand on the Sharpsburg Heights, "all our heavy baggage wagons, supply trains, etc., [began] filing through town to the heights" on the western outskirts of Sharpsburg, noted one Southerner. This, of course, clogged Sharpsburg's main thoroughfare "with ammunition wagons and ambulances."[161] From there, the ambulances proceeded west to deliver their bloodied loads to Shepherdstown. Following the crossing of the Potomac River back into Virginia, the gray-clad wounded made their

Open fields, like these near the Grove Farm west of Sharpsburg, provided ideal locations to treat the Confederate wounded during the Battle of Antietam. *Photographs of Civil War battlefields and cemeteries in Virginia, Maryland and West Virginia. MSS 12529. Special Collections, University of Virginia, Charlottesville, Virginia.*

Wartime view of Sharpsburg looking west along the Shepherdstown Pike toward Shepherdstown. *Library of Congress.*

way up the road running west from the ford and parallel to the river in the direction of Shepherdstown. Hence, the homes and churches on the town's eastern end felt the cruel hand of war before the rest of the town.

The home of Laura Parran Towner, whose family had already suffered from this war, was one of the first homes in Shepherdstown to receive the wounded. Just down the street from the Parran home sat another of the buildings first used as a hospital in town. This one, owned by the Schnively family, witnessed terrible and unforgettable scenes on September 15. Young Netta Lee remembered seeing her first wounded man in the Schnively house. The man had received a wound in his wrist, and as she entered the home, Netta Lee found the man being supported by two other soldiers as a surgeon attempted to pull the ball from his wrist. "He asked for water; I ran to get some," recalled Lee long after the blood had dried on the Schnivelys' floorboards. She returned and fanned the ailing soldier, who did not wince at his pain, "save once in a while a long breath and an 'ouch!'" Finally, the surgeon successfully completed the operation. "He never flinched or fainted; but, alas, I almost did and opened the door for air," remembered Netta Lee.[162] Indeed, the unexpected sight of scores of bloodied and mutilated men must have been a shocking sight for those who called Shepherdstown home.

The sights, smells and feelings that Netta Lee experienced in those opening hours of Shepherdstown's stint as a hospital seem to have been nearly universal among the town's populace. Another woman involved in dressing wounds became queasy from not only the sights of torn flesh but also the smells emanating from the wounds, an aspect one citizen called "fearful." The anonymous woman stumbled around upon completing her work, whereupon she clung to the railing of a staircase and muttered to herself in her "half conscious" state, "Oh, I hope if I faint some one will kick me into a corner and let me lie there!"[163] Unfortunately, the town was too full of helpless, mangled men for anyone to ignore its sights, sounds and aromas.

After their slave relayed the horrifying images of the Confederate wounded approaching Shepherdstown, the family of Mary Bedinger Mitchell rushed into town. There, they found "the streets already crowded, the people all astir, and the foremost wagons, of what seemed an endless line, discharging their piteous burdens." The scene stopped Mitchell in her tracks for a moment, "but fortunately we could not stay to look at it," she wrote, as work had to be done for these poor men. "There were no preparations, no accommodations—the men could not be left in the street—what was to be done?"[164]

Even though the sudden arrival of the entourage of wounded knocked Shepherdstown's citizens off their footing initially, they quickly regrouped and—whether driven by pure humanity, devotion to the Southern cause, or both—strove to provide the best accommodations possible for their guests. "Men ran for keys and opened the shops, long empty, and the unused rooms; other people got brooms and stirred up the dust of ages; then swarms of children began to appear with bundles of hay and straw, taken from anybody's stable," Minnie Mitchell fancifully wrote. Though it is inconceivable to think that these Confederate wounded moved unaccompanied by surgeons or nurses, the town went to work as if there were none.[165]

The jarring journey that exemplified a ride in a Civil War–era ambulance had undone most of the wound dressings these Southern men had originally received closer to the South Mountain battlefields.[166] The women of the town, who throughout this whole experience were especially commended by the Confederates they cared for, worked "with a devotion that went far to make up for their inexperience." They frantically searched for anything that could be construed as a bandage in order to dress the wounds of the injured men, "but what did they know of wounds beyond a cut finger, or a boil?" mused Minnie Mitchell when contemplating the enormity of their task.[167] Some of the women in Reverend Charles Wesley Andrews's home went so far as to sew shirts for as many of the wounded as possible.[168]

While Shepherdstown's men, women and children sought to find shelter and dress wounds as best they could, the professional surgeons of the Army of Northern Virginia continued their more grisly work. The women of the town provided comfort to the wounded and held the surgeons' instruments while "some amputating was done—rough surgery, you may be sure," remembered one of the residents. The quickly hardening hearts of the residents, caught up in this time of chaos, allowed them to conduct their tasks "nobly" as "the emergency brought out all their strength to meet it."[169]

Despite the large show of strength on the part of Shepherdstown's citizens, September 15, 1862, was already beginning to drain the town's resources. Reverend Andrews of Shepherdstown declared that those at his home were practically "eaten out" in those first few days.[170] Virginians living outside Shepherdstown poured supplies into the beleaguered village in the form of materials for bandages as well as food. However, "when all was done it was not enough," Mitchell wrote.[171] More and more wounded Southerners found their way into town and caused many anxious townspeople to wonder what they would do should more arrive or the wounded remain here for an extended period.[172]

Shepherdstonians began working extended shifts at the various hospital sites, even working late into the evening by candlelight. As sunlight replaced the burning wicks the next day, more injured Confederates arrived.[173] Some of the new arrivals were no doubt wounded soldiers who lagged behind in the previous day's retreat toward Sharpsburg. Others likely fell out of ranks and entered the town searching for food as soldiers crossed Boteler's Ford on their way from Harpers Ferry to unite with the rest of the Army of Northern Virginia at Sharpsburg. This double crossing of the ford—wounded men passing into Virginia and healthy men crossing back into Maryland—must have unnerved many of the healthy veterans moving toward an impending battle while also providing a microcosm of Lee's successes and failures in the campaign thus far: the success of the Harpers Ferry operation nearly muted by the disaster at South Mountain.

The increasing number of wounded in Shepherdstown brought more doctors, surgeons and nurses from the Confederate army with them. Minnie Mitchell recalled that, "with a few honorable exceptions," the doctors might as well have not even been in Shepherdstown to perform their duty.[174] It seems Samuel P. Moore's policy of examining all medical officers through the army medical boards had not yet been completely implemented. Physicians of the town such as Dr. John Quigley and the town's mayor Dr. John Reynolds joined in and offered any assistance they could.[175]

Despite being only a few miles from the front lines, Shepherdstown's residents had anything but a clear understanding of the campaign, leaving them mostly blind to the strategic results of the fights at South Mountain and Harpers Ferry. The soldiers passing near the town during their march from Harpers Ferry to Sharpsburg spread word of their victory but the current position of the opposing armies could not be gleaned from these same sources, though the distant boom of cannons reminded Shepherdstonians of their proximity to the battlefield. For as much relief—or anxiety—as this information created, the people of Shepherdstown were kept in a constant state of uneasiness knowing that some of their family members had been involved in the actions of the campaign. Surely, many a face must have looked heavenward praying that they would not recognize the face of a mangled soldier carried across the Potomac in an ambulance or on a stretcher.[176]

Whether or not they felt they had an accurate idea of the campaign's progress up to this point, one thing remained brutally clear in the minds of most of the men and women in Shepherdstown: the experiences that had befallen them so far might be only the first waves of a distant storm descending on their town. Like the thunder of a far-off storm, Shepherdstown's residents could

Sketch of Dr. John Quigley of Shepherdstown by Alexander Robinson Boteler. *Historic Shepherdstown Museum.*

turn their ears to the east and, on the evening of September 16, 1862, hear the prelude to the coming struggle. "As night drew nearer," Mary Bedinger Mitchell reminisced, "whispers of a great battle to be fought the next day grew louder, and we shuddered at the prospect, for battles had come to mean to us, as they never had before, blood, wounds, and death."[177]

On the front lines at Sharpsburg, those whispers amplified as rattling volleys of musketry and the low, terrifying sound of cannons engulfed the western Maryland landscape. As both armies jostled for position in the growing darkness of September 16 in the fields, orchards and woodlots outside Sharpsburg, Maryland, a sharp firefight ensued on the battlefield's northern portion in a stand of trees known today as the East Woods.

Compared to the fighting the following day, the firefight that broke out on September 16 between elements of the Northern and Southern armies was a mere skirmish in terms of its size. However, its intensity was a precursor to that of the larger Battle of Antietam on September 17. Casualties were minimal for a fight of such a severe nature, mainly due to its short duration, but they do not deserve to be overlooked in this, Antietam's prelude.

Perhaps the most well-known casualty—at least in the Confederate army—claimed in this fight was a thirty-six-year-old lawyer from central Mississippi.[178] A contemporary described Phillip Franklin Liddell as "a grand fellow" who "obeyed every order promptly and efficiently" and eventually became colonel commanding the Eleventh Mississippi Infantry, part of John Bell Hood's Confederate division.[179] On the evening of September 16, Hood's men were called into action to confront the Union thrust across Antietam Creek on the northern half of the battlefield. There, they clashed with the lead elements of the attacking Federals.

For its part, the Eleventh Mississippi mostly sat in reserve. However, its members did not escape unscathed as Federal shells screamed toward them and crashed among the ranks. In order to avoid as much of the fire as possible, Liddell instructed his men to lie down, a precaution he also followed, hugging the ground in front of his Mississippians. Suddenly, a shell burst above him, and a piece of shrapnel plunged into Liddell's body, leaving a gaping, bloody hole.[180] After the surgeons tried their best to patch up the wound and stop the flow of blood, Liddell became yet another mangled man sent across the Potomac River into Shepherdstown. There, he lay in his awful state in the chamber of Reverend Charles Andrews's home, waiting for his misery to end, which came nine days later.[181]

Darkness ended the fighting in the East Woods but left both sides with the knowledge that the next day's work would be deadly. Sensing such a struggle, Lafayette Guild sought more help. Writing from his "Camp opposite Shepherdstown"—perhaps from Ferry Hill Place—Guild requested James Herndon, the surgeon left behind at Manassas, to bring the ambulances and surgeons with him in northern Virginia to Shepherdstown by way of Winchester "so as to cross the Potomac River at that point [Shepherdstown]" and proceed to the wagon parks west of Sharpsburg. The medical director also instructed Herndon to hurry John Herbig's infirmary corps to the front. Guild did not only need more bodies to aid in the removal of the wounded, however. He also ordered Herndon to bring any medical supplies that he might find along the way.[182] If Guild got any sleep that night, it must have been brief, as he tirelessly worked to ensure that his medical corps was prepared for the next day's test.

View of Douglas Hill and Ferry Hill Place from the Maryland shore of the Potomac River. *Historic Shepherdstown Museum.*

Men along both lines of battle tried to steel their nerves as best they could for what they knew would come the next day: death, destruction and one of the hardest fights ever seen on the North American continent. Some surgeons prepared for their gruesome work in the German Reformed church in Sharpsburg and points farther behind the lines on that September night while others closer to the front contemplated the gravity of the situation and the dangers of their occupation.[183] Words similar to those written by Thomas Clark of the Fifth Florida at some point during the campaign must have resonated through many soldiers' minds that dark, quiet night as they turned their thoughts to their loved ones:

> *Farewell to you my darling*
> *Oh Farewell my dear.*
> *Do not weep for my long absence*
> *while I am present here.*
> *She wrung her little white hands*
> *and mournfully did cry.*
> *"You will go and be a soldier,*
> *and in the war you'll die."*[184]

6

"THE LONGEST, SADDEST DAY"

Antietam Overview

The Battle of Antietam began as the sun peeked over South Mountain on the morning of September 17. Union attacks began in the northern part of the battlefield around the East and West Woods and through a twenty-four-acre field of corn known today as The Cornfield. For the first hour of battle, one American fell every second as the two armies seesawed back and forth for possession of high ground near the Dunker Church. Gradually, Federal attacks shifted to the south toward a Confederate position in a worn-down farm lane, which the battle christened the Bloody Lane. After hours of desperate fighting, the Federals met success, but events to the south prevented a major breakthrough.

On the southern end of the field, Federal forces struggled across Antietam Creek at Burnside's Bridge. After a lengthy delay, these Federals connected with others who crossed the Middle Bridge on the battlefield and attacked Confederate positions east and south of Sharpsburg in an effort to cut off the Confederate army from its retreat route back into Virginia. The attacks nearly succeeded, but the defenders south of town doggedly held on until reinforcements from Harpers Ferry arrived and aided in turning back the Union tide.

The twelve-hour battle was a Union victory, although it came at the cost of 23,110 Federals and Confederates. Robert E. Lee found it impracticable

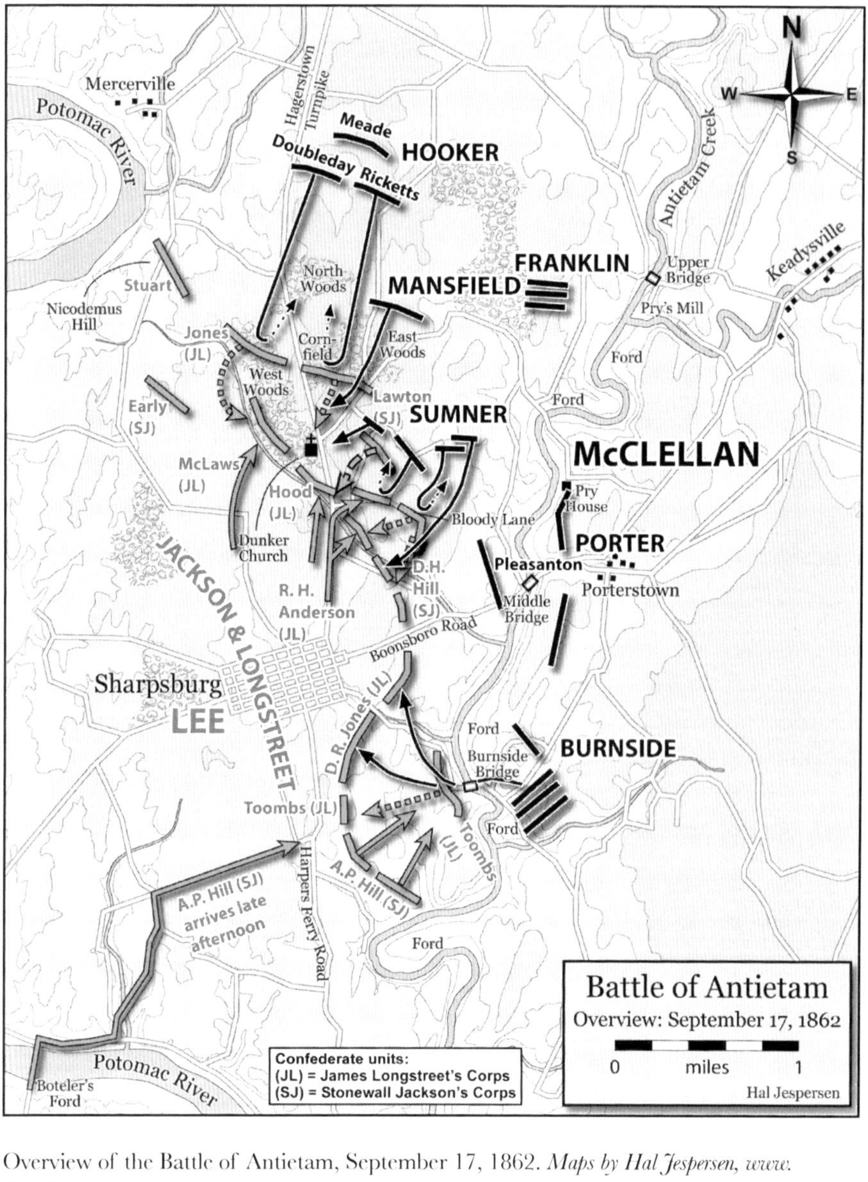

Overview of the Battle of Antietam, September 17, 1862. *Maps by Hal Jespersen, www.cwmaps.com.*

to retreat on the night of September 17. He held his ground on September 18 as both sides caught their breath from the bloodiest single day in American history. That night, Lee withdrew his army into Virginia one mile downstream from Shepherdstown.

"All in Confusion & Trouble"

The darkness of the night before the Battle of Antietam was impenetrable, although the scattered volleys of pickets on the front lines occasionally and unnaturally lit up the dark landscape. The flash of the rifle and the peculiar sound of the bullet whizzing through the air made the early morning hours of September 17, 1862, almost unbearable for the soldiers nearest the firing line. Soon, however, soldiers "could see the first rays of the sun lighting up the distant hilltops," and then all hell broke loose.[185] The light inaugurated one of America's darkest days.

The exertions of the previous two days had completely worn Shepherdstown's residents out. The early morning hours of September 17 gave them no additional time to rest. As sunlight began to illuminate the town, that far-away, dreadful noise of artillery fire startled Shepherdstonians from their sleep.[186] The residents of this previously quiet town were once again called to their bloody work, nursing their wounded guests.

The constant artillery and rifle fire coming from the direction of Sharpsburg gave the residents a clear idea of where their loved ones, friends and neighbors in the Confederate army were—there was no doubt of that now. Shepherdstonians did not have time to mull over the safety of those they held dear while the noise of battle "formed a background to our pain and terror," wrote a girl in the town.[187] Indeed, Charles Andrews correctly noted that should the Confederates "lines…fall back for one mile," Shepherdstown might be within distance of the Federal artillery. There was little time to think about this, however, as "the armies [were] all upon us with sick & wounded, & all [was] in confusion & trouble," Andrews continued.[188] The only option Shepherdstown's citizens had to keep the impending danger off their minds was to continue their ministrations to the wounded, a task that must have grown tougher and tougher as the battle raged throughout the day.

Although the wounded from South Mountain had already turned Shepherdstown into a large hospital, the numbers were "insignificant… compared to the tide of wounded that began to flow into the town early on the morning of the 17th."[189] With this in mind, an understanding of the fighting at Antietam, the Confederate medical corps' operations at Antietam, and the stories of Confederates wounded outside Sharpsburg who eventually made their way into Shepherdstown are essential to uncovering Shepherdstown's story as a hospital. It was not just the men, women and children of the town who had to endure terrible things; the soldiers also had to endure awful ordeals while being cared for in Shepherdstown.

A Surgeon's Battlefield

While Shepherdstown's committed citizens may have proved a godsend to the Confederate army and Lafayette Guild and may have aided in the recovery of some of the Southern soldiers who recuperated in town, another factor on the Antietam battlefield may have saved the lives of more wounded soldiers than students of the battle often give it credit: topography.

Studies of topography and terrain on a battlefield often fall into the trap of examining these important features on a large scale—such as the key terrain which an army had to hold in order to defeat their enemy—or examining how the terrain affected the decisions of generals on a battlefield.[190] Others, mainly geologists, have theorized how certain sedimentary formations underlying Civil War battlefields led to greater or fewer casualties, depending on which type of stone lay beneath the surface.[191] The rolling, undulating and deceptive terrain on the Antietam battlefield is often the focus of such studies. Antietam's terrain, however, not only played a role in the decisions of generals and in making some parts of the battlefield bloodier than others but also aided in saving the lives of many wounded soldiers, as well as facilitated their removal from the battlefield to safer points behind the lines, such as Shepherdstown.

Many rocky ridges and plateaus, upon many of which stood the Army of Northern Virginia in its defensive positions on September 17, characterize the Antietam battlefield. Deep, deceptive ravines intersecting and running between the battlefield's ridges allowed units to move from one point to another on the battlefield with ease while concealed from enemy view and protected from enemy fire. These same, subtle ravines, formed by the meandering tributaries and waterways flowing toward Antietam Creek, and prominent rock ledges also provided relative safety from the dangers of a battlefield for the assistant surgeons; "knapsack-toter[s]," who carried medical supplies to the front lines; and stretcher-bearers of the Confederate army, all of whom operated directly behind the front lines in field infirmaries. Here, wounded soldiers received initial treatment, which "consisted chiefly of the application of plaster and bandages and the administration of stimulants." Rarely was an "elaborate surgical procedure" seen at the field infirmaries "unless there was urgent necessity for it."[192] Following the receipt of first aid, the stretcher-bearers transported the wounded to a safer place farther to the rear at the regimental hospitals.[193]

Surgeons in Civil War armies did not have jobs as dangerous as those of assistant surgeons. Despite this, surgeons still found themselves close to—but not on—the front lines.[194] The regimental surgeons established their hospitals in "protected place[s] behind a hill or a gully," which were in abundance at Antietam and shielded most surgeons while they worked and spared wounded men from receiving any additional wounds. Regimental surgeons were responsible for "most of the major surgery of the war" at their hospitals, "particularly the amputations" if they found that such an operation was immediately required.[195] Wounded soldiers next journeyed even farther to the rear, usually via ambulance, toward the brigade- and division-level field hospitals, which were to be placed out of range of enemy fire and conspicuously marked by a flag.[196] At Antietam, these field hospitals were located in the farms, houses and barns west of Sharpsburg. Due to the limited number of structures in that area, Confederate surgeons also used Shepherdstown, which became the largest of these hospitals.

Even though the terrain and rock ledges on the Antietam battlefield might have made the work of Lafayette Guild's medical corps slightly easier, the sheer number of Confederate wounded they had to aid and collect offsets any advantages that these factors provided. Soldiers of both North and South felt that the fate of their nations rested in their hands at Antietam and that belief led to prolonged, vicious and particularly deadly fighting. Captain Henry Lord Page King, a Confederate staff officer, wrote of Antietam, claiming the July 1, 1862 "Battle of Malvern Hill was less severe in Artillery" while "no musketry of [the] war equaled" that seen at Antietam.[197] Surgeon James Boulware likewise said, "I pronounce this battle to have been the most terrible in artillery than any one of the preceding fights." He ended his diary entry on September 17 with the words, "I hate cannons."[198] Still another veteran of the battle remembered, "I have never witnessed more deliberate nor more destructive fire than that of this battle."[199] One Confederate general perhaps said it best: Antietam was "the hardest fought battle of the war."[200]

Miller's Cornfield—Lawton's Brigade

Marcellus Douglass paced back and forth behind his prone infantrymen, all eyes staring toward the corn. The orders resounded up and down the line: pick your "own corn row" and fire down it at the first sign of the enemy.[201] When blue-clad soldiers reached the southern fence line of the field, Douglass's Georgians rose up and poured a deadly volley into the Federals. The killing that would so characterize Antietam had commenced.

An early historian of the battle described the ferocity of this early part of the action: "At first no attention was paid by either line to the rail fence in their respective fronts, but each stood and fired on the other, neither party endeavoring to advance, soon, however, the severity of the fire dictated more caution and most of the men, on both sides, laid down and sought cover."[202] Men fell by the scores, and the number of wounded began to mount. The Battle of Antietam was only minutes old.

Among the wounded was Colonel Marcellus Douglass himself, who conspicuously moved behind his men throughout the fight, rushing "from regiment to regiment exhorting the men to hold their position, to shoot low, and make every cartridge count" despite his severe wounds.[203] Struck as many as eight times, Douglass finally succumbed to his wounds when a shell nearly separated him from one of his legs.[204] Despite the line's eventually falling back, Douglass's body remained in the hands of his men, who initially buried him near Shepherdstown.[205] The Army of Northern Virginia, however, carried many more wounded men to Shepherdstown than they did dead men from Douglass's brigade.

Douglass's Georgians suffered severe attrition among their line officers during their nearly hour-long fight. Lieutenant Colonel John T. Crowder, commanding the Thirty-first Georgia Infantry, was no exception to that rule. Like Douglass, Crowder put himself in the thick of the fight, constantly encouraging his men. While standing near the Thirty-first Georgia's flags, a Union shell found its mark in Crowder's breast; a moment later, a bullet to the abdomen knocked him to the ground. Fearing capture, Crowder urged his men to carry him to the rear. Two Georgians placed him behind a rock ledge for protection not far behind the line. The intensity of the fight, however, forced them to carry their commander "to a little church beyond the Potomac" in Shepherdstown. There, Crowder received some medical aid, though it was "poorly done at best," remembered one of the soldiers who carried him to Shepherdstown and beyond, where Crowder eventually recovered.[206] The citizens found no end to the stream of wounded that poured into their town on September 17.

Brigadier General Alexander Lawton, commanding the division, also could not escape the shower of Union bullets and shells converging on the gray-clad line south of Miller's cornfield. Lawton, a prewar cadet at the United States Military Academy, graduate of Harvard Law School, president of a railroad and member of the Georgia legislature, rode back and forth behind his lines, exhorting his men to hold their position.[207] Then, a bullet smashed into his leg, "passing between the two small bones below the knee," creating excruciating pain.[208] Lawton, too, soon found himself on a stretcher that carried him to Ferry Hill, the prominent estate overlooking Shepherdstown.[209] The men under Lawton's command—wounded or not—soon followed their commander to the rear, finally giving way under the relentless pressure George McClellan's Federals had applied. One member of Lawton's old brigade remembered the intensity of that fight and simply said of it, "our brigade was awfully mangled."[210]

Brigadier General Alexander Lawton. *From* The Photographic History of the Civil War.

Miller's Cornfield/Hagerstown Pike—Texas Brigade

Upon the retreat of Lawton's division, a reserve Confederate division moved out from behind the Dunker Church a half-mile south of the bloodied cornfield. These men from a host of states of the Deep South had, as one soldier recorded, "not eaten in three days, naught but green corn." Just as the campfires warmed their long-sought-after rations, "we were shelled and ordered into formation. I have never seen a more disgusted bunch of boys and mad as hornets."[211] The Georgians, South Carolinians and Texans, among others, soon found themselves advancing into a hornet's nest, directly into the teeth of their Federal opponents.

Twenty-eight-year-old Henry Julius Smith commanded Company D of the Hampton Legion from South Carolina. Smith, who had left an infant at home when he went off to war, was an attorney before he became a soldier.[212] Before deploying, Captain Smith and the rest of his comrades had to climb over a stout fence in order to organize in the open field south of Miller's cornfield. "Once over," remembered one South Carolinian, the men moved "like a hurricane…swept over the land."[213] Despite the harrowing fire, these stalwart men advanced north toward the cornfield.

As the Hampton Legion continued its advance, it soon came under a raking fire from its left. The command swung west in order to counter the threat.[214] Suddenly, the charging South Carolinians stumbled upon the stout post and rail fence, behind which they hunkered down, alongside the Hagerstown Pike, a mere fifty yards from the enemy. In this eye-to-eye combat, the Hampton Legion's colors fell four times while the unit lost more than half of its strength.[215] Included among the fallen was Captain Henry Smith, a bullet having pierced his heart.[216] Finding their position untenable, the Hampton Legion fell back, carrying as many of their wounded as possible with them to the rear.[217] Some of the wounded, such as Stephen Elliott Welch of the Legion, had to make their way back as best they could amid the tempest of bullets and artillery shells. Welch had been wounded twice, the second wound coming from a shell that, as he wrote, "knocked me stupid."[218]

Meanwhile, in the cornfield itself, a shell fragment crushed the foot of George Todd of the First Texas Infantry. While roughly 82 percent of his comrades fell in the cornfield—by now the thousands of bullets and tramping feet had cut most of the corn stalks—Todd limped his way to the rear to his brigade's field hospital. There, a surgeon told him the amputation of his foot was necessary, but Todd, in a unique scenario in Civil War hospitals, declined to part ways with his foot, promptly found an ambulance and made his way into Shepherdstown. He rejoined his regiment less than two months later.[219]

The slaughter thus far had been fearful for every unit—North and South—that had been in the fight. "Never have I seen men fall so fast and thick," remembered Stephen Elliott Welch of the Hampton Legion.[220] In the first hour of the Battle of Antietam, 4,368 men fell, a staggering 1.2 every second.[221] There were still eleven hours left.

"One Continual Roar of Thunder"

By 7:00 a.m., the fields and woodlots north of Sharpsburg were a confused mess. The litter of war—torn belts, cartridge boxes, ammunition chests and mangled muskets—mixed with the dead and wounded bodies of thousands of soldiers carpeted the ground with a horrifying display of war's consequences. Across the Potomac in Shepherdstown, the scene was equally chaotic and horrifying.

As the Battle of Antietam raged a mere four miles away, Shepherdstown's residents continued nursing the wounded who had already sheltered in their homes. During their brief respites from the grueling duty, some of the townspeople attempted to catch a glimpse of the action in Maryland. From the roofs of the town's taller buildings and from the hillside overlooking Boteler's Ford one mile downstream, the observers—both citizens and soldiers—found clouds of smoke obscuring much of their view.[222]

Despite the blinding blanket of smoke, Shepherdstonians perched on rooftops and hilltops easily experienced the audible elements of battle. One Confederate artilleryman camped on the property of Alexander Boteler, a Confederate congressman who lived one mile southwest of Shepherdstown, later recalled the noise of battle as heard four miles away on September 17:

> *At times the artillery fire was so fierce and heavy that it sounded like one continual roar of thunder rumbling and rolling across the sky. The musketry fire was equally severe and raged furiously, almost incessantly all day, and its hideous deathly crash vied with the deafening roar of the thundering artillery. It is utterly incomprehensible and perfectly inconceivable how mortal men can stand and live under such an infantry fire as I heard to-day. Judging from the way the musketry roared the whole surrounding air between the lines must have been thick with flying lead.*[223]

This ceaseless roar of battle surely must have been unnerving to even the sturdiest of souls residing in Shepherdstown. Yet the scene beneath the watching eyes of Shepherdstown's highly curious citizens did not stop because of the battle. In fact, it only grew worse.

Most of the Confederate wounded who found their way into Shepherdstown's streets and buildings on September 17 likely made it there themselves, as those wounded properly secured and transported by Guild's medical corps probably ended up being treated in the field hospitals established on the western fringe of Sharpsburg. Once they passed through or around the net of cavalrymen deployed behind the main line to prevent stragglers from leaving the front, the unwounded shirkers and "the wounded who were able to walk and look after themselves" came to the safe haven of Shepherdstown. Men were ferried across the Potomac River directly beneath the town and crossed the ford in such numbers that the capacity of Shepherdstown's buildings and the energies of its residents were stretching thin.[224] Archibald Atkinson, a surgeon in the army's cavalry branch, came upon his cousin's house—the Parran house—in Shepherdstown. There, he found that the home could not hold any more wounded men, which forced the Parran family to move some of them into the yard.[225]

Early on the morning of September 17, the flood of wounded men and stragglers already strained Shepherdstown's resources. The scene in the streets rivaled the chaos of the battlefield and left a lasting impression on all who witnessed it. Over two decades later, then twelve-year-old Mary Bedinger Mitchell still vividly remembered what she experienced in September 1862:

> *On our side of the river there* [was] *noise, confusion, dust; throngs of stragglers; horsemen galloping about; wagons blocking each other, and teamsters wrangling; and a continued din of shouting, swearing, and rumbling, in the midst of which men were dying, fresh wounded arriving, surgeons amputating limbs and dressing wounds, women going in and out with bandages, lint, medicines, food. An ever-present sense of anguish, dread, pity, and, I fear, hatred—these are my recollections of Antietam.*[226]

As the bloody work continued in the fields around Sharpsburg, Shepherdstonians' anxiety grew with each passing moment. The task of caring for wounded soldiers who seemed to be arriving every second kept them occupied for the time being, but the battle at Sharpsburg continued to provide traumatic background noise to the cries of the wounded.

Miller's Cornfield—Ripley's and Garland's Brigades

A mixed brigade of Georgians and North Carolinians became the next Confederate brigade to be fed into the maelstrom that was Miller's Cornfield. Colonel William L. DeRosset's Third North Carolina fought on the east end of the line near the East Woods. DeRosset, a native of Wilmington and former student at the University of North Carolina, led his men against the "well-formed ranks of the enemy, drawn up in three lines of battle and supported by artillery."[227] A gap soon developed in the Confederate line, and DeRosset moved his men slightly to cover the hole and face a charging Federal regiment.[228] The charging Yankees met the guns of DeRosset's North Carolinians, who temporarily stopped the threat.[229] However, the stand of the Tar Heels did not come without cost.

Sometime during this fierce firefight, two Federal bullets hit William DeRosset, one in his thigh and the other through his hip.[230] The painful wounds forced DeRosset from the field. The wound incapacitated him to such an extent that it became difficult to move the wounded colonel.[231] DeRosset's men eventually safely brought him to the rear, however.

On the other end of this Confederate formation, assistant surgeon William Proby Young of the Fourth Georgia busily worked in the discharge of his duties directly behind the Georgians' firing line. Young, a native Virginian and a graduate of the esteemed Jefferson Medical College in Philadelphia, was well respected by the men of the Fourth Georgia, who could entrust their well-being to him. Jovial, intelligent and brave, surgeon Young "never hesitated to go into the hottest fire on the field of battle in the discharge of duty." Clearly having the preferred characteristics of an assistant surgeon, Young would prove his willingness to work under fire on September 17. While aiding his wounded comrades yards south of the cornfield's southern boundary, Proby Young fell to the ground wounded. What he did next demonstrated a surgeon's devotion to his patients. When the Confederate line gave way to the Union onslaught, Young, despite his wound, remained on the field with the other wounded of his regiment and, while continuing to care for them, became a prisoner of the Army of the Potomac.[232] It would not be the last time on September 17 that a member of the Army of Northern Virginia's medical department became a casualty of war.

To the right of DeRosset's North Carolinians, another brigade from the Tar Heel State moved into the smoke-filled East Woods. This brigade, formerly under the command of Samuel Garland until his death three days prior, had been roughly handled by its opponents atop South Mountain and was jittery to enter another fight so soon. Commanders belched forth conflicting orders as the brigade approached the woods, and the fear of enemy movements on their flank broke the North Carolina soldiers. "A general panic ensued," noted the brigade's commander, and the gray-clad Carolinians streamed to the rear.[233]

During this brief fight south of the East Woods, James Atwell, commanding the Twentieth North Carolina's Company B, received a ghastly wound. A "heavy bullet" hit one side of Atwell's face "and passed out through the other side." Somehow, in the confusion of the moment, some of Atwell's men managed to extract his limp body from the battlefield. Atwell's mangled body eventually found refuge in the home of Daniel Rentch on German Street in Shepherdstown.[234]

West Woods—McLaws's Division

Coming from the south, the weary division under Lafayette McLaws witnessed a scene that must have shaken even the hardiest of veterans. As their well-dressed lines moved toward the sounds of battles, the horrific effects of battle came streaming toward them. Wounded men by the score passed through their ranks as the fields McLaws's soldiers advanced across were "being literally plowed and torn up by shot, shell and minie balls."[235] Near the right of the line, McLaws's trusted brigade of South Carolinians under Joseph Kershaw marched straight into the guns of the Federals.[236]

Kershaw's men from the Palmetto State charged out of the West Woods south of the Dunker Church directly into the mouth of the Northern guns situated on the high, open plateau opposite the church while the Federal infantry fled the scene in Kershaw's front.[237] "No sooner did we gain the top of the hill," wrote a member of D. Wyatt Aiken's Seventh South Carolina, "than they opened a most murderous fire of grape and shells from batteries on our right, front and left. Of all the cannonading I ever experienced, this was the most destructive. It seemed almost whole lines would melt away at once—still the cry was 'onward men, onward.'"[238] Urged forward by Colonel Aiken, the South Carolinains got to within thirty yards of the pieces and even temporarily captured some before being forced back.[239]

The destructive fire that the Seventh South Carolina encountered ended its brief foothold on the Dunker Church Plateau. "So rapid was the Federal fire of grape, Canister and Cannon balls of large size together with their Infantry fire, that we lost in Killed and wounded about three fourths of our number in fifteen minutes," remembered a member of Wyatt Aiken's Seventh Regiment decades later.[240] Upon falling back to the relative safety of the West Woods, Wyatt Aiken and several other men ducked behind a wood pile to avoid the Federal infantry and artillery fire—"a hurricane of balls," according to one soldier.[241] The cluster of soldiers determined to rally the unit in a ravine to the rear, and as they rose to go there, a ball struck Aiken in the left nipple, knocking him out of the remainder of the fight.[242]

Captain Thomas Hudgins of Aiken's unit found the colonel bleeding profusely, and fearing the wound to be life threatening, Hudgins brought Aiken behind the Confederate battle line and placed him behind a log for additional safety. Aiken, too, feared his life was ending and requested that Hudgins take his sword and return it to his family in South Carolina. The colonel's brother also found him, and the wounded commander instructed his brother to inter his body in Virginia and, once the war ended, reinter it in his native Palmetto State.[213]

Wyatt Aiken's brother and servant removed him to a field hospital in the rear, a stone barn belonging to the Reel family. A fellow soldier also seeking medical aid there saw Aiken and pleaded for a nearby surgeon to give some whiskey to the wounded colonel. However, the surgeon had none left—a ball put a hole through his flask and all of the whiskey drained out. "[B]esides," said the surgeon regarding Colonel Aiken, "he…will not live ten minutes."[214]

Farther north in the West Woods, the Thirty-second Virginia Infantry charged into the Union formation. The firing along the line—as it often did in the Civil War—produced thick, opaque black powder smoke and, with it, confusion. The Virginians came close to the enemy line but still could not locate its exact position. When a soldier in the ranks located the Federals and told his brigade commander, Paul Semmes, Semmes replied, "Yes, and they will kill the last one of us." Indeed, that seemed plausible, as the Thirty-second Virginia left the fight with nearly 50 percent of its members falling on the battlefield.[215]

Caught up in the maelstrom of Antietam, brothers Thomas and John "Jack" Barlow of Williamsburg, Virginia—members of the Thirty-second

Bedford, home of the Lee family of Shepherdstown. *Historic Shepherdstown Museum.*

Virginia—became victims of the deadly fire. Jack, a second lieutenant, received a bullet in the leg. His brother herded him off the field, and together—along with Lieutenant Robert Willis of the same unit—they wound up across the river in Shepherdstown at the home of Robert E. Lee's cousins, Bedford.[216]

Sunken Road

The sight must have been awe-inspiring to the Alabamians and North Carolinians hunkered down behind the fences bordering a little-known wagon road running northeast of Sharpsburg. There, quiet descended over the battlefield only briefly before the Southerners could make out the shouting orders of commanders on horseback and the high-pitched fife blending with the noise of the lower-pitched drum. Finally, the Confederates saw it: an impressive line of men dressed in Union blue, their guns carried at their hips preparing to charge the gray-clad defenders while the sun silhouetted their bodies perfectly for the Confederates in the road.

Colonel Francis Marion Parker commanded North Carolinians at the far right end of the Confederate line in the road. He wrote of those opening moments of the fighting at the Sunken Road: "I cautioned my men to hold their fire until I should give the command, and then to take deliberate cool aim; that I would not give [the] command to fire until I could see the belt of the cartridge boxes of the enemy, and to aim at these. They obeyed my orders, gave a fine volley, which brought down the enemy, as grain falls before a reaper."[217] Some of the most intense fighting to be seen on the North American continent began as the entire Confederate line erupted in a sheet of smoke and flame.

George Burgwyn Anderson commanded the Tar Heels in the Sunken Road. The thirty-one-year-old North Carolinian graduated from the United States Military Academy tenth in the class of 1852 and served in the prewar United States Army until the outbreak of hostilities between North and South.[218] A contemporary noted Anderson's "most marked traits…were his sincerity, his conscientiousness and his earnest devotion to truth." However, on America's bloodiest day, these "noble" traits would not save Anderson and his men from the storm of bullets flying toward the Sunken Road.[219]

Even well before the bullets began heading their way, the soldiers of Anderson's command knew that a hard-fought battle to their north was underway. Shortly after daylight, "we see the wounded come limping towards us," remembered John Gorman of the Second North Carolina.[250] At the Piper House, located behind the Sunken Road, a member of G.B. Anderson's staff recalled, "Soon after light the wounded from the Artillery commenced coming in, [and] pretty soon the wounded infantry came in by the dozens." Only one surgeon was present at the Piper home, but he and his assistants did the best they could for the stream of wounded men heading in their direction.[251]

Brigadier General George B. Anderson. *Library of Congress.*

Meanwhile, as the surgeons in the rear conducted their work, the frontline soldiers at the Sunken Road prepared their defense. George Anderson "occupied a prominent position on slightly rising ground, immediately in the rear of his command."[252] The fight at the road devolved into a test of courage as both sides tried to pour more lead at their enemy than what they could receive. This particularly took its toll on the Southerners in the road, who had only "about 6 or 8 inches of the wear of the road" for protection in some spots. "The protection, however, is not sufficient," noted a North Carolinian from his position in the lane. Sensing the dire situation, Anderson sent one of his aides to the rear to plead for reinforcements, "as it was hopeless to contend against the approaching columns."[253] Finally, Confederate reinforcements made their way toward the road, though many were shot down before reaching it.

The Florida Brigade was one of the brigades sent to Anderson's assistance, although Virginians and Alabamians also constituted this mixed command. The regiments of the brigade were "cut to pieces" and "were badly cut up in one hour's time," reported a member of the brigade. The Fifth Florida lost five color-bearers in the action. Positioned in the center of the brigade, the Fifth and Eighth Florida regiments were subjected to "a murderous fire for about one hour," leading to high casualties in both units.[254]

Thomas Clark of the Fifth Florida received two painful wounds, one in his leg and the other in the breast. Clark was transported to a home in Shepherdstown, where "he was well cared for."[255] Bird Wright of the Eighth Florida also made his way to Shepherdstown following his wounding at the Sunken Road, where "a ball entered my left shoulder and lodged in my breast where it still is," he wrote four days after the battle.[256] The Federal firepower was wreaking havoc not only on the Confederates rushing to the lane, however, but also those inside the roadbed.

The approaching blue lines continued to make it hot for the Confederates in the Sunken Road. "The air is full of lead," wrote Lieutenant Gorman, who received a wound while lying in the road. The wounded were so numerous, he thought, that he could hear their groans "amid the roar of the musketry."[257] George Anderson's voice could also be heard despite the din of battle, as he showed "the most splendid courage animating his men by his example, and directing them by his cool and collected orders." While displaying himself conspicuously, a ball entered Anderson's foot "near the ankle-joint," thus knocking him from his feet.[258] To move from the Sunken Road, especially while wounded, was "certain death," remembered one Confederate, but the general had to be removed to the rear.[259] "He was at once carried with difficulty and danger" to a hospital near the Piper farm, where the undulations of the ground partially shielded him from the fighting. There, "the wounds [were] examined and pronounced severe but not serious," recalled a member of his staff.[260]

Later, when the Federals broke through the Confederate defense at the Sunken Road, they came within "30 yards of the [Piper] house," according to one account. Anderson, fearing capture, convinced three members of his staff "and two other men of the Ambulance Corps" to carry him farther behind the lines. Together, the men placed him on a stretcher and "carried him through a field that looked like it was impossible for [a] man to walk ten steps without being killed," but they somehow all made it to the rear alive, though one man was slightly wounded by a Federal artillery shell.[261] The stretcher-bearers proceeded to put the wounded general into an ambulance and find a more protected place well out of range of the Federal guns where Anderson's surgeon could better examine the general's wound.

Cemetery Hill—Evans's Brigade

Far from being a surgeon, Nathan "Shanks" Evans was still known throughout the Army of Northern Virginia—or at least among the soldiers under his command—as always being one to help a wounded man. Wielding "a small two-quart cask of liquor" he affectionately called his "barrelita," Nathan Evans never let a wounded man pass by him "without a draft upon its contents…[S]everal times at Sharpsburg, was it emptied and refilled," noted an eyewitness.[262] Evans became widely regarded throughout the army as "the best drinker, the most eloquent swearer (I should say voluble) and the most magnificent bragger," according to one man.[263]

Despite these personality traits, Shanks Evans seems to have had a bit of a friendly side to him. Willoughby Farquhar Trezevant, a "mere lad," attached himself to Evans's staff following the wounding of one of his brothers and the death of another earlier in the war. Only seventeen years old, Trezevant quit his studies at South Carolina College—present-day University of South Carolina—and eventually "came to Virginia, hoping to be able to avenge these double injuries." Evans found that the boy possessed "great intelligence" and made him his "little Secretary." Throughout his service to the general, Trezevant "was ever to be found close to the General's side."[264]

Poised atop Cemetery Hill all day on September 17, Evans, his staff and the men under his command constantly found themselves ducking and dodging to prevent falling prey to the iron that Federal artillery was shooting toward them from ridges to their front and those across Antietam Creek. At one point, the firing was so intense that Evans turned to the adolescent Trezevant and told him to head to the rear out of the range of the Federal pieces. A newspaper correspondent present at the scene reported Farquhar Trezevant's supposed stoic response: "No, General. I don't want to go back—I want to see the fight, and be by your side." Shortly thereafter, a shell came whistling in Evans's direction, and it struck Trezevant, positioned directly behind the general. "His leg was completely taken off," Evans told his wife two days later.[265]

Farquhar Trezevant's wounding took place just north of the direct road from Sharpsburg to Shepherdstown, and the mortally wounded boy was very quickly transported along that thoroughfare to the hospitals on Sharpsburg's west end. Probably on September 18, the boy was moved in a wagon and carried to the home of Charles Wesley Andrews in Shepherdstown. At age seventeen, he may have been one of the youngest casualties of the Battle of Antietam.[266]

Harpers Ferry Road—D.R. Jones's Division

The fading afternoon sun poured over the backs of the obstinate gray-clad defenders positioned south of Sharpsburg poised to meet the next Union thrust. For the men of the tremendously depleted Seventeenth Virginia Infantry, holding on to that ground before the assault even began strained the nerves of even the most solid veteran.

Federal artillery to the east rained shot and shell on the Confederate defenses. "[T]he air around us grew resonant with the bursting iron," recalled a member of the Seventeenth Virginia, which sought shelter as best it could behind a post and rail fence. "A shell burst not ten feet above the Seventeenth," continued the soldier, which "literally tore to pieces" one man, "mangling his body terribly and spattering his blood over many who were lying around him."[267]

In an attempt to deal with the murderous artillery fire, Captain James S. Brown's Wise Artillery wheeled into line next to the Seventeenth. Working among the guns was "a volunteer for the occasion": Dr. William S. Parran.[268] During the fight, Dr. Parran "fell shot through the head" before the battery pulled out of line. He was probably killed instantaneously or nearly so, and members of William Crenshaw's Virginia Battery recovered Parran's remains. Captain Crenshaw, who "seems to grieve as much as if he [Parran] was a near relative," conveyed the body back to Lillie Parran and her sisters and mother in Shepherdstown.[269]

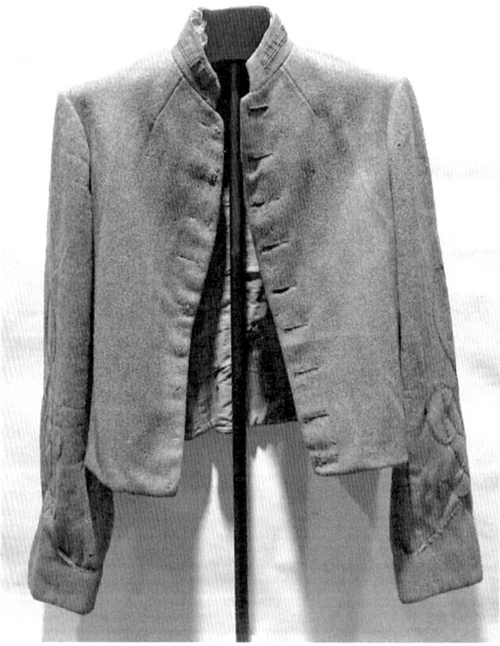

Coat of Lieutenant Francis B. Littleton, Seventeenth Virginia Infantry, who died in Shepherdstown on September 25, 1862, from wounds received at Antietam. He is buried in Leesburg, Virginia. *Virginia Military Institute.*

Meanwhile, once the Wise Artillery moved to the rear, "an ominous silence followed, premonitory of the deluge."

The Confederates behind the fence could make out the shouting commands of Federal officers and the clattering of accoutrements and canteens—the sign of men on the move. Suddenly, the flagstaffs came into view, then the Stars and Stripes, men's hats and, finally, a perfect line of blue-clad soldiers. At sixty yards, the Seventeenth Virginia and the other units positioned atop the ridge let loose a thunderous volley. Despite the initial shock of the volley, the Confederate line could not hold back the tide for long, as the Federal forces traded volley for volley with their opponents. Shortly thereafter, the gray-clad troops melted to the rear "without order or formation."[270]

In testament to the ferocity of the fighting along this sector of the line, William J. Hall of the Seventeenth Virginia received four wounds in the short amount of time his regiment fought. All feared that Hall would not survive. His companion, Edgar Warfield, remembered that after placing Hall on a stretcher, the seven survivors of his unit "knelt by the side of the litter…and offered up a prayer." Warfield removed Hall to a barn in the rear "and remained with him all night."[271]

"In the Midst of the Wounded and Dying"

Darkness brought a close to "a battle surpassing all others of the war in the numbers engaged and its intensity," recorded one soldier. "The day had closed, but what a scene presented itself to our view! The dead lay in every direction—in numerous places piled on each other," he continued. Finally, he labeled September 17, 1862, "the longest, saddest day."[272] As the din of fire receded toward the end of the day, the more awful cries and groans of the wounded filled the evening air.

While the debris of war littered the ground north, south and east of Sharpsburg, that to the west perhaps witnessed some of the worst scenes of the night. Men along both lines slumped into a deep sleep wherever they happened to be, utterly exhausted from the day's fighting. One Southern general remembered watching the lanterns flicker across the dark landscape like so many fireflies in the night—the medical corps, as well as everyday Confederate soldiers, were searching for survivors.[273] Captain William Stores of the Thirty-second Virginia Infantry received permission sometime in the battle's wake to venture back to where his regiment fought in order to care for the wounded and bring as many of them to the hospitals as possible. With a handful of men, Stores proceeded on his mission of humanity. During the trek, he encountered General Lee, who inquired where Stores and his group were heading. Stores explained his mission, and Lee softened his voice and told the captain, "Well, get them to the nearest hospital as soon as possible, and then join your regiment. My men are very much scattered."[274] The dispersion of Lee's men made the task of collecting wounded that much more difficult for Guild's surgeons.

Due to the size of the battlefield and the immense number of casualties, collecting and caring for all of Antietam's wounded was no simple task. In addition, the ferocity of the action—as previously discussed—led to an unusual number of severe wounds. A surgeon with the Sixth South Carolina recorded in his diary of this phenomenon: "The wounds generally in more of a serious nature than heretofore."[275]

In order to coordinate the operations of the Confederate medical corps during perhaps its toughest test to date, Lafayette Guild left his headquarters opposite Shepherdstown and spent most of the day around the Grove and Smith farms along the Shepherdstown Pike west of Sharpsburg.[276] Besides Shepherdstown, these farms and the fields around them became the central Confederate hospitals behind the army's lines.[277] Supposedly, at the Grove farm, also called Mt. Airy, 1,400 soldiers were hospitalized. "A great rough-hewn table was used for amputations" and discarded arms and limbs were buried on the Grove property.[278] A Georgia newspaper correspondent described the scene at one of the hospitals behind Confederate lines: "I write at a hospital, in the midst of the wounded and dying,

Dr. Hunter Holmes McGuire, chief surgeon of Stonewall Jackson's command. *From* The Confederate Cause and Conduct in the War Between the States.

amputated arms and legs, feet, fingers, and hands cut off, puddles of human gore, and ghastly, gaping wounds."[279]

Such scenes were becoming more and more commonplace in Shepherdstown, also. Despite the majority of Confederate wounded arriving in Shepherdstown on the night of September 18–19, evidence suggests that Lee and Guild began removing the wounded from Maryland on the night of the battle. All the wounded able to be moved were forwarded to Shepherdstown, some by ambulance and others under their own power.[280] Dr. Hunter McGuire, chief surgeon in Jackson's command, supervised this retrograde movement.[281]

The Battle of Antietam produced an estimated 10,316 Confederate casualties, including about 7,752 wounded.[282] Despite the large disparity in numbers between wounded and the number of surgeons to care for them, most accounts praise the actions of the surgeons in gray on the Antietam battlefield. In the First Georgia Regular Infantry, assistant surgeon William

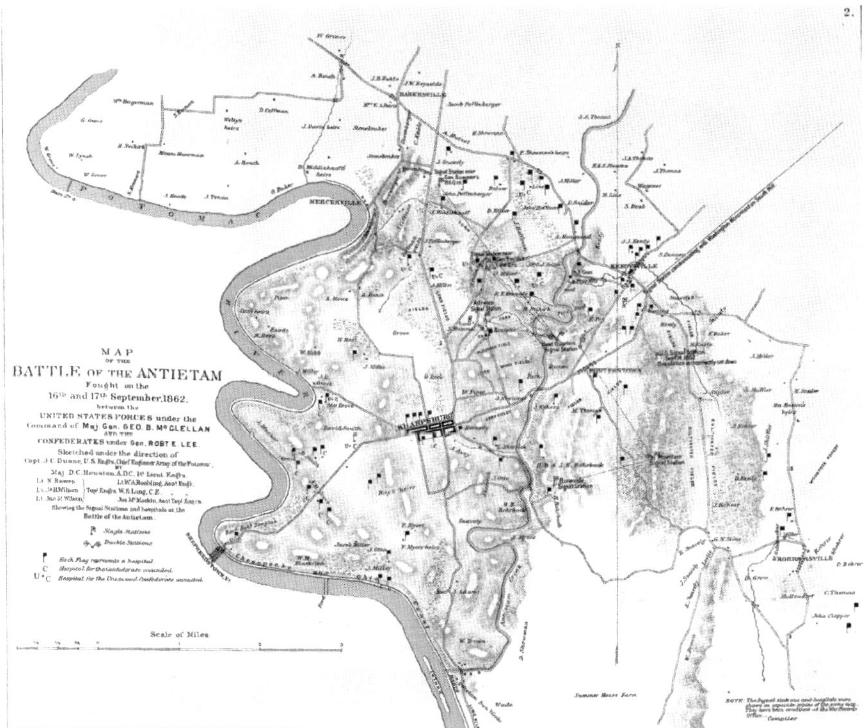

Map of the hospitals surrounding the Antietam battlefield. Each flag represents a hospital site. *From* Atlas of the War of the Rebellion.

R. Bickers lost the horse he was sitting on while trying to bring wounded soldiers to the rear.[283] James Longstreet commended his chief surgeon, James Cullen, and his associates for their "active and unremitting…care of the wounded, and," continued Longstreet, they "have my thanks for their humane efforts."[284] War, however, is anything but humane, and despite their best efforts, Guild's medics could not prevent the deaths of every wounded Southern soldier.

From a Confederate perspective, the Antietam battlefield—like any battlefield, for that matter—turned out to be dangerous for many surgeons and wounded men despite its advantageous terrain and availability of shelter because, as the Confederates ceded ground to their antagonists, places that had been safe for Confederate wounded in the morning were no longer appropriate places for field infirmaries by the afternoon, such as with the case of George B. Anderson at the Piper farm. Perhaps even more revealing is the story of the hospital at the Reel farm, located west of the Piper homestead.

The Reel barn following the fire that consumed it—and many of the Confederate wounded sheltered there—during the Battle of Antietam. *Library of Congress.*

The large bank barn owned by David Reel provided an ideal location for a hospital—it had plenty of space for the wounded and sat sheltered behind a prominent ridge. However, once Confederate infantry and artillery established their fallback positions atop the ridge, overshoots from enemy artillery began to drop in among the wounded. "The fire of the Federal Batteries on this point was terrific," remembered one of the wounded there. Eventually, the wounded man calculated the firing pattern of the guns and slowly moved his way toward Sharpsburg in between each volley. "I final[ly] got off some hundred of yards toward the Town, I looked back, and saw that the Barn or building had been fired, and suppose some of our wounded were burned to death."[285]

Indeed, in one of Antietam's most tragic stories, the flames consumed many of the wounded inside the Reel barn, as townspeople digging through the ruins after the battle "found lumps of lead of several pounds where bullets had been melted that were carried by soldiers who were supposed to have been burned in the barn. They also found portions of bones of human beings in the ashes," remembered an early historian of the battlefield.[286] Unfortunately, this would not be the last time in the Maryland Campaign that wounded men and surgeons became subjected to the shrieking and bursting of artillery shells. When the Army of Northern Virginia left the Antietam battlefield in its wake on the evening of September 18, it placed Shepherdstown and its citizens squarely in the path of war and of those same deadly projectiles.

7
"LIKE AN AWFUL DREAM"

For twelve hours on September 17, from sunup to sundown, Shepherdstown's residents had worked amid the booming of the guns some three miles distant, giving the battle the sound of an incoming storm. Indeed, it seemed that a storm of sorts was on its way to Shepherdstown—a storm that its residents had tasted since September 15. However, the storm that came the next two days after the Battle of Antietam was such that hardly anyone could have expected it.

When the sun set on the bloodiest day in American history, Shepherdstown's residents could peer across the Potomac and glimpse "innumerable camp-fires," all the while imagining "the scenes that they were lighting. We sat in silence," remembered Mary Bedinger Mitchell, "looking into each other's tired faces. There were no impatient words, few tears; only silence, and a drawing close together, as if for comfort. We were almost hopeless, yet clung with desperation to the thought that we were hoping. But in our hearts we could not believe that anything human could have escaped from that appalling fire."[287] Despite the ferocity of the fighting that Wednesday, September 17, thousands did manage to evade death, a fact Shepherdstonians realized the next day when those men began pouring into the town.

By midnight of September 17, thousands of wounded turned Shepherdstown into "one great hospital."[288] Any building where "four walls and a roof were found together" became a makeshift hospital. Accordingly, doors were thrown open, and homes, warehouses, stables and churches—to

Postwar view of Shepherdstown's drill room (third building from the left), which was supposedly one of the first buildings to house Confederate wounded. Moulder Hall is the last building on the right in the row of buildings. *Goldsborough/Surkamp Collection.*

name a few—housed as many wounded as could be comfortably fitted.[289] Even though they seemed unnecessary in a place where every building was transformed into a place of recuperation for first hundreds and then thousands of Confederates, hospital flags were run up on most of Shepherdstown's buildings, the first reportedly being the old militia drill room on King Street. Soon, Confederate surgeons moved more wounded, and their headquarters, into neighboring Moulder Hall.[290]

Moulder Hall is one of the more remembered hospitals in Shepherdstown. Local legend holds that it witnessed the more serious operations, namely amputations. "There were many amputations of arms and legs [in Moulder Hall], and the surgeons, grown callous by much work of this sort, performed their duties in a mechanical sort of way," says one postwar account. "At one corner of the building was a pile of feet and legs and at the other a collection of arms that had been amputated."[291] Though this may certainly have been the case at Moulder Hall, it does not seem likely that only one building was used for amputations, especially in a town filled with several thousand wounded.

As September 17 turned into September 18, the town continually received more of its unexpected guests, and the buildings were filling to capacity. Indeed, at Dr. John Quigley's home on German Street, at least thirty-four soldiers found refuge inside, while others "lay upon the porches or in the yard."[292] Sarah Page Andrews, Dr. Andrews's wife, sat at her parlor window, gazing out into the streets filled with ambulances while wounded men lay along the sidewalks.[293]

Fortunately for Shepherdstown, not all of the approximately 7,700 Confederate wounded arriving in the town would stay for very long, if they even stayed at all.[294] If a wounded soldier could walk or bear the jarring ambulance ride, the army's medical corps sent him directly to Winchester and points beyond, particularly Staunton and, eventually, Richmond. For one of these ambulatory wounded men, Winchester was typically a day's trip from Shepherdstown, then five days to Staunton, followed by a daylong trip on the rails to the Confederate capital.[295] Despite many wounded Confederates taking this option, at least several thousand men temporarily called Shepherdstown home in the days immediately following Antietam.

The wounded who arrived in Shepherdstown from the Antietam battlefield arrived in myriad ways. In order to escape from the dangers of the battlefield, soldiers used any means necessary to make their way to the hospitals on the south bank of the Potomac. A wounded colonel found a horse hitched to a barn, stole it and made his way toward the river.[296] Another soldier from Mississippi had his slave impress the services of a Sharpsburg farmer's horse so that he could get across the river and avoid capture.[297]

Colonel Wyatt Aiken of the Seventh South Carolina also found transport to the river after two men carried him the three miles or so to the base of Douglas Hill opposite Shepherdstown. There, Aiken and his aides used a method of crossing the river that harkened back to the days when the ferry business boomed on the Potomac River at Shepherdstown. A canoe was obtained—or impressed—into service and carried the wounded Aiken into the hospital town during the dark night of September 17.[298]

Aiken was not the only Confederate to use boats at the ferry landing to reach the Virginia shore. One account noted the "superhuman efforts" required "to ferry the hundreds of wounded across the stream."[299] For a brief moment, the activity at the ferry landing must have reminded Shepherdstonians of the peaceful times before the war. However, the constant stream of bloodied soldiers entering their homes and buildings quickly dispelled such thoughts.

Most of the wounded making their way toward Shepherdstown used Boteler's Ford, located one mile downstream from Shepherdstown, which they reached by either using the Shepherdstown Pike until its intersection with the Chesapeake and Ohio Canal towpath and then following the towpath to the ford or cutting across the country through the fields of the Grove farm. Once crossing the "deep & rocky" ford, soldiers and teamsters worked their way up a narrow road running along the Virginia bluffs crowning the river almost the entire distance to Shepherdstown.

The road—and the ford, for that matter—seemed incapable of handling so many men, horses and wagons. A Confederate veteran remembered after the war that the road leading from the ford to Shepherdstown "was so narrow that a horseman…could not easily pass a wagon" and "a few wagons wrecked would block the road completely at many points."[300] In addition, the riverbanks at the ford were steep, which made entry and exit from the river no easy task, particularly for wagons. A Southern newspaperman succinctly summed up the difficulty of the area for such a movement to his readers. Following a description of the narrow road and the cliffs bordering it, he wrote, "Thus, you perceive, the character of the Virginia side was almost as unfavorable as it could be to the safety of the [army's withdrawal]."[301] The terrain—chief among other factors—made the Confederate crossing of the wounded and the army at Boteler's Ford particularly difficult.

Whether the wounded of the Army of Northern Virginia who crossed the Potomac on September 17 into the morning of September 18 did so of their own volition or under orders is unclear, but what remains clear is that by the afternoon of September 18, Robert E. Lee had begun preparations for a withdrawal into Virginia. The army's immense wagon trains and the wounded they carried went first.[302] Once the retrograde movement commenced, the problem of transportation reared up and continued to plague Lee's army. Enough wagons could not be spared to carry all the wounded into Virginia, meaning many of the injured Southern soldiers had to be left behind, especially those unable to endure a jarring wagon ride or escape under their own power.[303] The exact number Lee left behind will never be precisely determined but easily rests among the thousands. Jonathan Letterman, Lafayette Guild's counterpart in the Army of the Potomac, calculated that he and his surgeons had to care for about 2,500 Confederate wounded from the battles fought at South Mountain and Sharpsburg.[304]

While some of the wounded who fell into Union hands knowingly did so, others fell behind—or were left behind—accidentally. Despite removing his wounded to the field hospitals west of Sharpsburg, General Jubal Early reported, "Some 10 or 15 of my wounded were left in a hospital on the Maryland side of the river when we recrossed…by some mismanagement on the part of the surgeons or quartermasters."[305] Others, likely due to the lack of transportation or the nature of their wounds, had to be left behind. In many cases, Confederate surgeons volunteered—or suffered the short end of the draw—to remain with the soon-to-be-captured wounded.[306]

Wagons were the main source of transportation that brought Confederate wounded to Shepherdstown. *From* Battles & Leaders of the Civil War.

Many wounded, aware of their impending capture, found any means possible "to place the Potomac between themselves and the enemy." One account estimated this procession of walking wounded at several hundred.[307] A member of this ghastly procession noted, "All along the road were men with an arm, a hand, or a finger amputated, yet trudging forward, determined not to be left in the enemy's hands."[308] This same fear of being wounded and becoming captured played out in Shepherdstown the following day.

For those well enough to bear a ride in an ambulance to Shepherdstown and points beyond, the three-mile journey proved to be anything but easy. Rain soaked the roads and wagon wheels, horses and marching men turned the thoroughfares into a quagmire.[309] The army slowly trudged its way through the mess, often passing by the tormenting scenes of hospitals established along the roadside. "I often shuddered at the sights and sounds thereunto appertaining," remembered one witness.[310]

The movement of the wounded—followed by the rest of the army—to Boteler's Ford was slow, chaotic and oftentimes painful. Lee's immense wagon trains stretched end to end from Sharpsburg to the Virginia side of the Potomac.[311] The Shepherdstown Pike "was perfectly crowded with artillery & wagons," not to mention the cavalry and infantry also using that road to reach the ford. A large, stop-and-go, bumper-to-bumper traffic jam is perhaps the best comparison to the Army of Northern Virginia's movement into Virginia on the night of September 18. It was so bad, in fact, that one soldier recorded moving at the glacial pace of one mile every one and one half hours.[312]

To make matters worse, the night was "dark & foggy," and "the darkness was so great," remembered one Confederate staff officer, "that one knew not where to direct his doubtful steps."[313] This, coupled with the nature of the roads due to the rain, and the logjam that characterized Lee's withdrawal into Virginia, made the nighttime march "some of the most tiresome and fatiguing work it was ever the lot of an army to do."[314] For the wounded soldiers riding in uncomfortable, bumpy ambulances, the march must have been much more awful. Yet the path from Sharpsburg to the Maryland shore of the Potomac was the easy part of their journey.

Upon reaching the riverbank, wagon drivers had to maneuver their loads "down a very high and almost perpendicular bank," which was "such a descent as no prudent wagoner would ever have attempted to make" in a less pressing situation. The descriptive soldier continued, "the teamsters had to make an elbow [turn] half way down, at the imminent risk of an overturn," which happened on several occasions.[315] At one point, an ambulance spilled over and crushed one man caught beneath it.[316]

Once the wagons conquered this tricky piece of maneuvering, they plunged into the ford and the "inextricable confusion in the water," much of which was "full of large bowlders [*sic*]." Tremendous bonfires—meant to illuminate the ford—emitted enormous amounts of smoke, worsening the difficult crossing for driver and animal alike. "Altogether there was a terrible racket," remembered one participant.[317] The nature of the ford and the hurried situation again contributed nothing to making the journey for wounded and healthy soldiers alike any easier.

At least several ambulances were unable to move through the rocky and deep ford. In fact, the water was so deep at points that it "came up several inches into the ambulances." Tired, fatigued and cranky soldiers trudging through the water forced one ambulance out of the ford and into even deeper water, where it became "wedged in the rocks." Edgar Warfield, in charge of the Seventeenth Virginia's wounded, called for aid and, only after some difficulty, freed the ambulance.[318]

Toward midmorning on September 19, the end of the army's immense trains and columns finally reached the Virginia shore. The march's conclusion produced one of the more memorable stories relating to Shepherdstown's tenure as a Confederate hospital. Maxcy Gregg's South Carolinians were the last to cross back into Virginia. As Gregg and his men entered the river, they came upon an ambulance full of wounded Southerners. "The cowardly driver had unhitched his horses, crossed the river, and had left his suffering comrades to the mercy of the foe," wrote one eyewitness. Fearing capture,

A milldam standing just upstream from Boteler's Ford. Confederates also used this to reach Virginia during the withdrawal across the ford. *Library of Congress.*

"the poor fellows begged piteously to be carried to the other [Virginia] side." Maxcy Gregg called upon his soldiers to help the wounded men reach the Old Dominion. Twelve or so men sprang forward to the task, "laid hold on the ambulance and pulled it through the water, in most places waist deep," while bystanders welcomed the men into Virginia with the tune "Carry Me Back to Old Virginia."[319] Lee, his army and most of his wounded were now temporarily safe, with a barrier between them and the enemy.

From Boteler's Ford, the Army of Northern Virginia ascended the steep Virginia bluffs and made its way into Shepherdstown. There, the wounded comingled with the host of wagons, civilians and stragglers filling the narrow streets.[320] From Shepherdstown, those well enough to withstand another arduous ride proceeded to Winchester, approximately thirty miles away. One of the soldiers responsible for transporting wounded from the ford to Shepherdstown and points farther south remembered using an ambulance belonging to the Second Rhode Island Infantry—a testament to the number of captured United States Army ambulances that saw service in the Southern armies.[321]

To this point, the sudden arrival of hundreds—soon thousands—of wounded had been a major disturbance and burden for Shepherdstown's residents. However, September 19 marked a watershed, as the experience truly became a nightmare for the town. The increasing inundation of unexpected guests was beginning to tax the town's resources and energy, but as more and more wounded arrived, Shepherdstown tried its hardest to meet this awful demand.

By the morning of September 19, wounded Confederates filled each of the town's six churches, "the Odd Fellows' Hall, the Freemasons', the little Town Council room, the barn-like place known as the Drill Room, all the private houses after their capacity, the shops and empty buildings, the school-houses—every inch of space," remembered one of the residents.[322] Already, two to three thousand Confederates huddled in any available space, longing for medical care.[323] At her home, Bedford, Netta Lee found Alexander Lawton occupying her brother's room, Rooney Lee the room next to Lawton and the Barlow brothers of the Thirty-second Virginia in another room of her home. In the room directly next to hers, Lieutenant Robert Willis of the same unit lay dying. Fortunately for the Lee family, the Southern surgeons whisked Lawton and Rooney Lee—both of whom survived—away relatively quickly to safer points, but Netta Lee and her family still played host to the other wounded left in town.[324]

The arrival of more and more wounded prompted Shepherdstonians to think of any structure—complete or not—that could provide some protection from the elements. They next flung open the doors of the recently constructed, but still not completed, town hall. The empty interior was resolved by placing "a few rough boards across the beams, placed piles of straw over them, laid down single planks to walk upon, and lo, it was a hospital at once." Buildings that had been closed for years, such as the Old Mecklenburg Warehouse at the water's edge, were thrown open, hastily prepared and occupied by the never-ending procession of wounded men.[325]

One of the enduring pieces of local lore in Shepherdstown history holds that during this period, the only building in town not used as a hospital was the Trinity Episcopal Church, which, according to the legend, served as a "hospital for the soul."[326] However, no contemporary evidence supports this—indeed, the primary accounts almost overwhelmingly claim *all* of the town's churches became hospitals. Furthermore, it seems highly unlikely that the Episcopal

Above: Shepherdstown's Presbyterian church served as one of the town's largest makeshift hospitals. *Historic Shepherdstown Museum.*

Right: Wartime image of Shepherdstown's town hall, one of many public buildings used as a hospital. *From* Prominent Men of Shepherdstown.

church, one of the larger buildings in town, would have remained empty while wounded men lay in the streets, exposed to the elements.

The Episcopal church's reverend, Dr. Charles Andrews, played host to Colonel Phillip Liddell of the Eleventh Mississippi—wounded on September 16—and Nathan Evans's aide, Farquhar Trezevant.[327] On the day of the Battle of Antietam, Dr. Andrews expressed grave fear that the wounded already in the town would eat his family out of house and home.[328] In the following days, the Andrewses conducted a full-scale operation at their home to provide for their guests. "We keep two pots on the fire all the time," wrote the reverend's wife, Sarah. She and others dealt tomato soup "to the sick & indeed all who apply," including the large numbers of men who bunked on Shepherdstown's streets. The young girls of the town joined in to help, providing aid that included sewing shirts for the threadbare Rebels.[329]

With their buildings filled beyond capacity and Shepherdstown's residents worried for their own welfare and safety, another colorful incident serves to demonstrate the burden that the several thousand wounded Confederates placed on Shepherdstown's citizens. While the Confederates desired much food, they also sought, and found, another staple of human life: water.

The hot summer days of September 1862 parched the tired, worn-out soldiers of both the United States and Confederate armies. In Shepherdstown, several pumps made fresh water available to the passing Confederates. "There was always a crowd around the town pumps, which were kept going continuously," said one resident. "Some of the men, fevered by their wounds and almost perishing from thirst, could hardly drink enough to satisfy."[330] So many men utilized the pump known as Grant's pump that its supply waned and "drew up only muddy water." A member of the Rickard family—a famous family of whitesmiths, one of whom produced John Brown's handcuffs in the wake of his Harpers Ferry raid—stepped forward to save the town's fresh water supply.[331] Elijah Rickard, seeing the impending calamity, "brought forth a short chain and one of his own dependable locks," moved through the crowd of soldiers, "and calmly proceeded to lock the [pump] handle close to the wooden stock," thus making the pump no longer operational. Initially, the parched soldiers expressed some irritation at the closing of a source of water, "but the sight of the quaint old man defying an army was too much for the boys in gray, and they could only laugh and cheer him as he manfully held his ground." Rickard, closely monitoring the pump, subsequently removed his famous lock once the water supply was replenished.[332]

While Shepherdstown's residents tried their best to provide the comforts of home to Lee's wounded soldiers, they ultimately could not protect them

Shepherdstown's various pumps provided fresh water to the Confederate wounded in the town, who almost bled this supply dry. *Historic Shepherdstown Museum.*

from the harsh realities of war. Shortly following the completion of Lee's withdrawal across the Potomac, Federal cavalry and artillery reached the banks of the river and perched themselves atop Douglas Hill, where they unlimbered several batteries of artillery and opened fire on any moving Confederate targets within range and eyesight. Unfortunately, Shepherdstown, which for days had heard the sounds of distant artillery, now fell victim to the raining iron belched forth from the mouths of the Federal guns.

Randolph Shotwell of the Eighth Virginia remembered well the first shells to land among Shepherdstown's streets on September 19. As he was sitting in a doorway, a Shepherdstown woman approached him with a slice of pie in one hand and a glass of buttermilk in the other. Suddenly, a gun boomed from across the river and the shell landed "near a church full of wounded." Startled, the matron dropped the plate of pie and fled to the cellar of her home.[333]

Elsewhere, at Bedford on the outskirts of town, shells passed over the home's east wing throughout the two-day Battle of Shepherdstown (September 19–20). One of the Lees' slaves was scared "out of her senses" by the shrieking shells, despite the failure of at least seven of them to explode.[334] Another story noted how the Federal guns "fired whenever they saw anything moving," and when they did, "the shell's [*sic*] knock[ed] off chimneys and occasionally [went] through the houses."[335] The very thing Shepherdstown had averted in December 1861 now became a reality. War was truly at its doorstep. Wounded men filled its homes, marching armies maneuvered through its streets and battle raged across its fields.

Understandably, the shelling of Shepherdstown caused a considerable deal of panic among both the citizens of the town and the Confederates—the wounded and healthy alike. "What before was confusion grew worse; the retreat became a stampede," concluded Minnie Mitchell. The distant thunderstorm, which Shepherdstonians had heard for the last several days, now hovered directly above them. "It is curious how much louder guns sound when they are pointed at you than when turned the other way," Mitchell wrote.

In an effort to show the Federals they were shelling mostly noncombatants, Shepherdstown's residents began to display yellow cloth over their homes in a vain attempt to stop the Federal fire. However, this measure failed to accomplish its goal, and the shelling continued. The Federal guns, as Mitchell correctly noted, were not aimed at the town itself but at the Confederate army moving beyond and outside the town. As a result, "most of the shells flew over us and exploded in the fields," if they exploded at all. Some shells did fall dreadfully short, though, for as Mitchell again astutely said, "aim cannot always be sure, and enough shells fell short to convince the terrified citizens that their homes were about to be battered down over their ears."[336] What followed was a scene of utter chaos in Shepherdstown's streets and buildings.

Indeed, despite the barrage of Shepherdstown being accidental, the town did suffer considerable damage from the raining iron missiles. Mitchell recalled entering the old factory building at the corner of Princess and High Streets to aid the wounded "when a shell crashed through a corner of the wall and passed out at the opposite end of the building…The wounded screamed," she remembered, "and had they not been entirely unable to move, not a man would have been left in the building." Though it was a narrow escape, no one inside the building received additional injuries, even when another shell struck the building later. Elsewhere in town, a small schoolhouse filled with helpless wounded felt the impact of an enemy shell, as did several other buildings in town.[337]

Even before Shepherdstown inadvertently came under fire, most of the wounded did not intend to be there for long. They knew the town's proximity to the United States Army and knew the longer they lingered, the higher the chances of their capture. A postwar Shepherdstown newspaper article best captured this natural impulse. "There was an irresistible desire on the part of the wounded soldiers to get further away from the scene of battle and find safety at Winchester and other points on south, and so those who were slightly injured would have their wounds dressed here and away they would trudge along the roads leading southward," it said.[338] When the shelling of the town began though, able wounded men joined unarmed residents of Shepherdstown in fleeing to a safer area.

The mass exodus from Shepherdstown produced an unimaginable scene in the town's streets and environs. "The road was thronged; the streets blocked," recalled Mitchell. She continued: "Men were vociferating, women crying, children screaming; wagons, ambulances, guns, caissons, horsemen, footmen, all mingled—nay, even wedged and jammed together—in one struggling, shouting mass."[339] The peaceful though disheartening scene that Sarah Page Andrews witnessed earlier from her parlor window—the streets clogged with ambulances, wagons and men—had changed dramatically. Many of the Confederates huddled amid Shepherdstown's streets and buildings began to flee the area once the bombardment began. Soon, rumors that eventually turned out to be true of Federals crossing the Potomac at Boteler's Ford spread through the town, and the soldiers, fearing capture, ran to the countryside and to points farther south to evade their enemy.[340]

General George B. Anderson, wounded at the Sunken Road, was one such wounded man removed from the dangers of possible capture or death by the approaching Federals. Following his wounding on September 17, doctors on the Maryland side of the river examined his ankle and determined his wound was "severe but not serious." The medical corps brought him across the river to Shepherdstown, where he found refuge in the stately home of the Boteler family.[341]

There, Margie Boteler consoled Anderson's wife in North Carolina. Writing from the general's bedside, Boteler informed Mrs. Anderson that her husband's wounds were not severe. Furthermore, she wrote, "He means

Remains of the Boteler home, Fountain Rock, following its burning by Federal troops in 1864. *Historic Shepherdstown Museum.*

to make his way to you very soon."[312] The bursting of Federal shells and fears of the enemy crossing the Potomac and capturing the wounded in Shepherdstown fueled Anderson's anxiety to return home. Due to his wound, many believed he should remain in Shepherdstown, "but he [Anderson] revolted at the idea of falling into the hands of the enemy, and his heart yearned for the ministrations of his devoted and lovely wife, and the endearments of his infant boy."

Like many other Southern wounded, Anderson proceeded from Shepherdstown up the Shenandoah Valley by wagon to Staunton, where he caught a train to Raleigh, North Carolina. Following the weeklong journey, George Anderson found himself in the comforts of his family.[313] However, Anderson's wound became more painful, perhaps an effect of the arduous trip home. His physician soon discovered that rather than the projectile glancing off his ankle—which everyone believed had been the case—the ball had become embedded in his ankle. The wound soon became infected, necessitating amputation, and George B. Anderson died of infection in his brother's home on October 16, 1862.[314]

Most of the Confederate wounded who initially found shelter in Shepherdstown trod south on the Valley Pike to reach Winchester and Staunton. *Cedar Creek and Belle Grove National Historical Park.*

Once out of Shepherdstown, the Confederate wounded who left both before and after the errant Union shells began landing in the town made Winchester their next stop. Utilizing the Valley Turnpike running the length of the Shenandoah Valley, these men passed through an area already touched by war. Its rich and fertile farms had been denuded by the soldiers who had passed through the area in the spring, and they now looked even worse as the procession of wounded passed through. One Shenandoah Valley newspaper wrote of "these poor, ragged, toll-worn, battle-scarred heroes trudging wearily and painfully along" the Valley Pike.[315]

By the next day, September 20, the refugees from the Army of Northern Virginia had reached Winchester. Mary Greenhow Lee, a resident of the Shenandoah Valley town, wrote in her diary that day: "The streets have been crowded with ambulances bringing in thousands of wounded men & I have been going all day to the Hospital." Though she knew that she could only make a small contribution—"a drop in the ocean," as she called it—she, like many of Shepherdstown's residents, consoled herself in the fact that her sacrifices and contributions showed that "some poor men were comforted."[316]

Nearly one week after Winchester's sudden inundation with wounded Southerners, one member of the Confederate medical department estimated that as many as six thousand wounded soldiers had arrived in the town. "Even the sidewalks of the streets are full of wounded," he said and, echoing a recurring problem throughout the Army of Northern Virginia, noted the "great scarcity of surgeons" available to treat the multitudes of wounded men.[317] During that time, Lafayette Guild worked to impress "neighboring barns or buildings" around Winchester that were "sufficiently commodious" for sheltering the army's sick and wounded. After moving as many of the sick and wounded away from Shepherdstown as possible, Lee ordered Guild to proceed to Winchester to "organize this [medical] department for efficient action."[318] Guild did the best he could under the circumstances, leaving only those unable to bear the trip to Winchester in Shepherdstown.

The Federal bombardment of Shepherdstown on September 19 did not scatter all the wounded from the town. Though most fled to safer territory within days, if not hours, of their arrival, an estimated eight hundred to one thousand wounded men, "among them a considerable number of officers, some of whom were men of highest standing and character from the far South," said a postwar edition of the *Shepherdstown Register*, remained in Shepherdstown.[319] Unfortunately, some of them would never leave.

One of the first Confederates buried in Shepherdstown was, in a way, a native of the town. After Dr. William Parran's body reached Shepherdstown, his aunt, Laura Towner (formerly Parran before she remarried), did her best to give her nephew "a decent burial."[350] However, in times of war, such ceremonies are hard to come by. Laura and her daughters, including Lillie, laid their family member's remains to rest "with the aid of several negro men" in one of the town's many cemeteries, where he still rests today. The crude ceremony took place during one of the Federal bombardments of the town, a cruel irony paralleling Parran's service with the Confederate artillery at the time of his death.[351] William Parran left behind a wife, an infant daughter and, at the time of his death, a yet unborn son.[352] In one of his last letters home to his family, William Parran wrote a note to his baby daughter. It read, "Daddy's little Emma—must be a good girl and know her daddy when he returns."[353]

September 19 marked the climax of Shepherdstown's experience during the Maryland Campaign. During the day, perhaps as many as six thousand sick and wounded Confederates attempted to plant themselves in the relative shelter of Shepherdstown's streets, homes, warehouses and churches.[354] Even though only approximately one-sixth of the wounded remained in town over the following weeks and months, Shepherdstown still faced the realities of war. "I hope all this will pass away like an awful dream in a short time," wrote one resident on September 18. "[W]e try to do our duty for the time, & trust to Providence for the future."[355] Though Shepherdstown had passed through the worst part of its tempest, what the future held in store for it remained unclear as the two contending armies continued to linger about the area, separated by the very river that Shepherdstown sat high above.

8
"I SHUDDER EVEN NOW, IN RECALLING IT"

While September 19 proved to be one of Shepherdstown's most traumatic days, it did not mark the conclusion of its trying hour. For days, weeks and even months following the arrival of the Army of Northern Virginia's wounded, the shelling of the town, the subsequent chaos and the Confederate evacuation of most of their wounded, Shepherdstown remained caught between two hostile armies while still playing host to a considerable number of wounded men. Even worse for the town, the next day, Saturday, September 20, brought a continuation of the fighting at Boteler's Ford; only this time, the fight was more deadly and intense than that of the previous day.

The shelling of Shepherdstown on September 19 resulted from the pursuit of the withdrawing Confederate army by Alfred Pleasonton's blue-clad cavalry troopers and, later on, Union infantry led by General Fitz John Porter. Prior to the battle at Shepherdstown, Porter, some of whose guns may have erroneously fired on the citizens of Shepherdstown, was blamed by Confederates for opening fire on a Confederate hospital north of Richmond during a battle the previous May.[356] Porter seemed to have a reputation for firing on hospitals, at least in the biased eyes of Southerners. While the Federal guns hurled shells across the Potomac on September 19, Confederate guns in Virginia replied, and a daylong artillery duel commenced across the river.

By late evening on September 19, Porter "determined to clear the fords, and, if possible, secure some of the enemy's artillery" posted on the Virginia

Major General Fitz John Porter. *Library of Congress.*

bluffs guarding Boteler's Ford.[357] Those guns that Porter coveted belonged to Episcopal minister turned soldier William Nelson Pendleton. The fighting parson commanded forty-four guns and approximately six hundred worn-out infantry, all of which scattered when Porter sent several hundred men across the ford at dusk.[358] In a frenzied panic, much like Shepherdstown just hours before, William Pendleton rode to the rear in search of help and finally stumbled upon Robert E. Lee's headquarters. Pendleton then presented Lee with very disconcerting news: the enemy had captured all forty-four of his guns.[359] Lee, no doubt concerned of a possible Federal incursion into his rear, ordered his trusted lieutenant Stonewall Jackson to turn the enemy back.[360]

Brigadier General William Nelson Pendleton. *Library of Congress.*

Meanwhile, on the Maryland side of the Potomac, Porter, buoyed by his success, proposed a reconnaissance of the Shepherdstown area the following day and began to cross his infantry early on September 20. Once inland, Porter's men ran into the lead elements of Lee's returning army and began to fall back to the bluffs overlooking the Potomac, where several dozen of their guns could provide support.[361] Confederate infantry under the command of Ambrose Powell Hill advanced into the teeth of the powerful Federal artillery while attempting to expel their blue-clad foes from the Virginia shore. Moving forward in two lines, Hill's infantry faced one of the most severe cannonades of the entire war. In addition, it also had to endure Federal infantry fire.

Though small in nature, the two-day Battle of Shepherdstown did not fail to produce gruesome scenes of horror found on numerous Civil War battlefields. Andrew Wardlaw of the Fourteenth South Carolina witnessed Lieutenant James Dunlap of his unit get torn in two by a shell.[362] A Northern newspaper correspondent watching the gray-clad soldiers advance under

The Battle of Shepherdstown occurred atop these Virginia bluffs. *Photographs of Civil War battlefields and cemeteries in Virginia, Maryland and West Virginia. MSS 12529. Special Collections, University of Virginia, Charlottesville, Virginia.*

such a fire surmised that the Southern loss "from our artillery fire must have been heavy, as the explosion of our shells was seen to make large gaps in their lines."[363] Another Confederate serving in the Twenty-second North Carolina Infantry recalled the "perfect hail of bullets" he and his comrades encountered upon getting within range of the Federal rifles.[364] The battle "was gruesome—distressing," recalled one veteran, who admitted years later, "I shudder even now, in recalling it."[365] This brief but intense fight lasted only a couple hours before Hill's Southerners forced Porter's troops to withdraw back into Maryland. The Maryland Campaign was over.

The fighting at Boteler's Ford took place only one mile from the heart of Shepherdstown. On Saturday, the second day of fighting, Shepherdstonians continued to fear for the fate of their town as cannons and muskets roared on its outskirts.[366] In addition to the continued fear brought by more fighting, the Battle of Shepherdstown brought a "few more wounded to town," noted one resident.[367] Though these additional patients arrived in only a trickle compared to all those who came from the fighting at Sharpsburg, they were in no better shape.

Artillery fire often produced tremendously horrific wounds. For many of the Confederates who participated in the fighting at Shepherdstown, they witnessed the serious nature of artillery wounds and soon brought that realization to the residents of Shepherdstown and the outlying area. J.H. Garrett of the Fourteenth South Carolina suffered such a wound. The regimental surgeon J.H. Powell kept a notebook that provides a window into the workings of a Confederate surgeon in the Maryland Campaign; in it, he describes Garrett's operation: "Had both legs mangled[.] [I]t was decided to amputate above the knees. Chloroform having been administered one leg was removed, patient so exhausted that it was deemed impossible to continue. Brandy administered freely—no reaction; died two hours after the operation."[368] Garrett became one of many Confederates whose lives were lost in the little town of Shepherdstown in September 1862.

While many Southerners—both soldiers and civilians—fled Shepherdstown on September 19, many other soldiers continued to receive care at the hands of Southern physicians and Shepherdstonians following the conclusion of hostilities along the banks of the Potomac. It seemed as if the ceasing of large-scale fighting in the region brought about an air of peace and friendship over Shepherdstown—at least as much as could exist during times of war. Indeed, as Union excursions constantly passed through town in the weeks following the Maryland Campaign, they often found Confederate wounded "walking the streets of Shepherdstown" as if there were no war at all.[369]

The Confederates who remained behind in Shepherdstown following the mass exodus of September 19 almost came to call the place their home. Indeed, many Shepherdstonians seemed to treat them as long-lost relatives due for a visit. Whenever possible, the town's residents attempted to provide as much comfort as possible to the wounded in their homes as well as to the families of the injured men. Thomas Clark, a member of the Florida Brigade who had been dangerously wounded at the Sunken Road, received such personal care.

Painfully struggling through two wounds suffered at the Battle of Sharpsburg, Thomas Clark lingered in Shepherdstown for nearly two months following the fight. Clark initially believed he would recover and make it home to his wife, as his caretaker in Shepherdstown recorded. However, after uttering this, Clark "got steadily worse thereafter and died." As a final memento, Clark's caretaker sent his wife a lock of her husband's hair and tried to put into context the reasons for his premature death. "I sympathize with you very much in the loss of your Husband, but he died in a glorious cause fighting bravely for our Independence." Clark's body, among scores of others, was laid to rest in Shepherdstown.[370]

Shepherdstown resident Daniel Rentch. Captain James B. Atwell, Twentieth North Carolina Infantry, died in Rentch's home on October 12, 1862. *From the* Shepherdstown Register.

While some of Shepherdstown's residents had to write letters home for the wounded men, some soldiers remained strong enough to do so themselves. Often, they urged family members to visit them and bring them home. Bird Wright, another Floridian, told his wife to come to Shepherdstown or, if she could not make it, tell his brother to make the trip. Wright even gave detailed directions to his wife regarding how to reach him.[371] Whether any of Wright's family members ever made it to Shepherdstown is unknown, but if they did, they likely did not find him alive. His personal records never conclusively close the case, but lists his reason of absence as follows: "Left at Shepardstown [*sic*] Sept 19, thought to be mortally wounded[.]"[372] His family likely never concretely knew—though they almost certainly guessed—that Wright probably died in Shepherdstown and was subsequently buried in an unmarked grave.

Soldiers' attempts to bring their families to the front lines and aid in their recovery did not always end in neither party knowing the other's fate. As the days of September wore on, the case of James Atwell of the Twentieth North Carolina became more severe, prompting his father to come to Shepherdstown several weeks following Atwell's injury. The weeks preceding this meeting had been tough for Captain Atwell. Resting in the home of Daniel Rentch on German Street, Atwell's facial wound began to recover slowly, revealing him as "a fine gentleman and a remarkably handsome man."

Upon his father's arrival, however, "the wounds reopened, hemorrhage set in" and Atwell died on October 12, 1862. Before his death, James Atwell and his father spoke of going home to North Carolina. Now, Atwell would be "taken home, indeed, but as lifeless clay and not as a hopeful, living son eagerly anticipating his father's house."[373] Such was the tragedy that Shepherdstown bore witness to in the late summer and fall of 1862.

Some soldiers' families came not just to Shepherdstown to visit their wounded relatives but also, if necessary, passed on to Sharpsburg to see their captured relatives left behind in the precipitate retreat. Under flags of truce, both armies permitted such an occurrence.[374] Lafayette Guild also utilized such understandings to check on the Confederate wounded still in Sharpsburg under the care of the Federal surgeons. However, rather than being fearful of Federal surgeons mistreating their Southern prisoners, Guild continually received reports of the ineptitude and carelessness of the Confederate surgeons who remained behind with their wounded.

In response to these reports, Guild ordered one of his surgeons "to proceed…to Sharpsburg and the neighbouring [*sic*] hospitals and make as thorough an investigation of the truth of this report as will be permitted you." He further instructed the surgeon to "ascertain the condition and wants of our wounded left in Maryland."[375] In most cases, Guild's worries were likely unfounded. Evidence suggests that Confederate surgeons worked

Union pickets stand opposite the Virginia shore at Boteler's Ford following the Maryland Campaign. *Library of Congress.*

Edwin Forbes's sketch of the Grove farm following its occupation by Federal forces. Note the wounded Confederates lying around the house. *Library of Congress.*

President Abraham Lincoln and numerous Union officers pose in front of the Grove farm following Lincoln's visit to Confederate wounded there on October 3, 1862. *Library of Congress.*

Jonathan Letterman (seated, left) medical director of the Army of the Potomac. *Library of Congress.*

alongside their Union counterparts to aid the wounded of both sides following the Maryland Campaign, though either side could not always avoid mistreatment of wounded prisoners.[376] Either way, medical director of the Army of the Potomac Jonathan Letterman believed, "Humanity teaches us that a wounded and prostrate foe is not then our enemy" and expected every one of his surgeons to adhere to that principle.[377]

Lafayette Guild had to look after not only his surgeons and the wounded of his army left across the Potomac but also those on the river's southern shore. Numerous accounts of the Confederate hospital in Shepherdstown imply, whether purposefully or accidentally, that the only people who cared for the gray-clad soldiers were the men, women and children of the town. Furthermore, these accounts, except for a few passing references to Confederate physicians, almost exclusively disregard the Rebel surgeons who remained in Shepherdstown to look after their own wounded. In reality, these accounts strike far from the truth, for a considerable Confederate medical corps presence existed in

Shepherdstown even following the evacuation of many of the wounded on September 19.[378]

As stated earlier, Lafayette Guild established his headquarters opposite Shepherdstown in the days leading up to and encompassing the fight at Sharpsburg, already suggesting a Confederate medical corps presence in the town. While Guild supervised the operations closer to the front lines, he ordered the Louisiana surgeon William A. Carswell to "take charge of sick & wounded at Shepperdstown [*sic*] during the battle at Sharpsburg." Guild lauded Carswell's actions performed under the "pressing exigencies" that existed at Shepherdstown. He further elaborated on the difficulty of Carswell's position, which "under the circumstances compelled him to perform not only the duties of Surgeon, but those pertaining to the Quartermaster & Commissary's Dpts."

Guild wrote this praising letter in late November 1862, at which time he believed the hospital at Shepherdstown still required Carswell's—and the rest of his medical corps'—attention. Guild and Carswell relieved some of the surgeons assigned to the hospital in Shepherdstown as early as the first week of October.[379] No record exists of when Carswell rejoined the main body of the Army of Northern Virginia, but other records indicate a Confederate medical presence in Shepherdstown as late as January 1863.[380]

Alexander Tinsley never intended to become a doctor. A recipient of a bachelor's degree in philosophy from the College of William and Mary in 1852, the native Virginian moved to Alabama to teach. While there, Tinsley aided in nursing victims of a yellow fever epidemic, an experience that inspired him to become a medical practitioner.[381] Tinsley obtained a medical degree from the University of the City of New York and held several surgeon positions prior to following his native state into the Confederacy. The doctor initially served in a hospital on the York-James Peninsula before serving with the Army of Northern Virginia.[382]

Arriving in Shepherdstown days before the Battle of Antietam, Tinsley used the Parran home on German Street for his headquarters. While staying there during the Maryland Campaign and in the period following its conclusion, Tinsley caught the eye of Mary Dare Parran, "a beautiful and charming girl who was one of the many noble women of [Shepherdstown] who devoted themselves to the care of the Southern soldiers." The two later married and, following the war, settled in Shepherdstown.[383] This relationship did not blossom overnight, however, as Tinsley remained behind with the Confederacy's wounded soldiers until January 1863.[384]

Dr. Alexander Tinsley in 1863. *Special Collections, Swem Library, College of William and Mary.*

During his extended stay in Shepherdstown, Tinsley, as well as the rest of the Confederate wounded remaining in the town, worried over the prospect of capture by the enemy. The Federal army was hopeful of capturing as many of those left behind in Shepherdstown as possible, especially following the surrender and subsequent paroling of nearly thirteen thousand Union soldiers at Harpers Ferry on September 15. The quicker a similar amount of Confederates could be captured, the sooner those Harpers Ferry Federals could be returned to the war's front lines.[385]

Union cavalry forays into Shepherdstown and the surrounding countryside occurred almost daily following the conclusion of the Maryland Campaign on September 20. One on September 29 netted anywhere from four to six hundred wounded Southerners, who were subsequently paroled by the reconnoitering Unionists.[386] During another trip across the river, a blue-clad cavalryman had the opportunity to see Shepherdstown. "The place had the appearance of one immense hospital," he remembered. As they rode through town, the Federal horsemen found men of their own army, who were captured during the late campaign and held temporarily in Shepherdstown. These former prisoners were subsequently conveyed back across the Potomac on boats, the same means used by the Confederates to transport a number of their wounded into the small Virginia town.[387]

Robert E. Lee claimed on October 8 that about 4,500 of the wounded from the Maryland Campaign had safely made their way to Staunton and were thus out of range of Federal raids. The sick and wounded who fell into the Federals' hands at Shepherdstown, Lee wrote, were "principally composed of stragglers" who came to the town for "repose and refreshment." Lee further claimed that the wounded who did temporarily reside in town "were transported before they were exposed to capture, except such as could not bear transportation, and had to be left to their fate." The general proved unhappy over this outcome, as he noted that his army was now relegated "to exchange [enemy] prisoners of war to release men who have done us no service."[388] However, as has been seen, many of the Confederates paroled in Shepherdstown had performed a great sacrifice for their country.

Both the armies of the Confederacy and of the United States agreed upon the system of parole during the early stages of the war, which held that paroled prisoners could not take up arms in the conflict until an equivalent number of the enemy had been paroled. Many of the Southerners captured in Shepherdstown experienced this limbo-like life following the Union treks into the area.

Postwar view of Shepherdstown's German Street and the Entler Hotel. *Historic Shepherdstown Museum.*

David Wyatt Aiken of the Seventh South Carolina had taken up refuge in the Entler Hotel on German Street at the time he was paroled. Aiken, nursed by his brother and Ella Harper, a local resident, slowly recovered from his wounds, despite reports back home of him having been mortally wounded.[389] Aiken's parole ended in January 1863, but that did not mean he could fight again. The wound held him out of the war until June 1863, when he rejoined his comrades. Aiken was with his men during the Gettysburg Campaign but afterward "was deemed unable for further active service in the field," upon which he was discharged. Following the war, he found a calling in politics and served five terms as a Democratic member of the United States House of Representatives before dying in 1887.[390]

Similar to Wyatt Aiken's, the wounds that others had nursed during their stay in Shepherdstown proved to be life changing. For Colonel William DeRosset of the Third North Carolina, his wounds proved so debilitating that he "lived a cripple for life," according to one fellow North Carolinian.[391] DeRosset's division commander smartly predicted that DeRosset's serious wounds to his hip and thigh would "forever deprive the South of his most valuable services," at least in the field.[392] DeRosset, like many others, never fully recovered from the horrors he experienced during the Civil War.

Still others who recuperated in Shepherdstown spent some of their last days of service in the army as convalescents in a town turned upside down. William J. Hall of the Seventeenth Virginia received four wounds at the hands of his enemy at Sharpsburg. His companion Edgar Warfield managed to place Hall in a wagon during the Confederate retreat from Sharpsburg, and after a difficult journey, Warfield placed the severely wounded twenty-two-year-old boy in "a vacant storeroom." Warfield, one of the few uninjured men in the Seventeenth, subsequently left Shepherdstown with the rest of the army, leaving Hall behind.

Following Warfield's departure, someone saw Hall's wounds and placed a sheet over the injured boy. "On it they pinned a card giving his name and regiment and requesting that whoever buried the body would please mark the spot," related Warfield in his memoirs. A lady from the town passing through the hospital then happened to catch her hoopskirt on Hall's stretcher, which roused it enough to awaken the wounded boy, who let out a groan from underneath the sheet placed over him denoting the hopelessness of his recovery. The Shepherdstonian and her companion took Hall into their home upon discovering his condition and brought him back to health, though he could never rejoin the army.[393] The wounds did not stop Hall from continuing to serve his country, however. Upon being discharged due to the injuries to his arms, including the paralysis of one, Hall served in the Confederate Post Office and after the war went into a business partnership with the man who had brought him back into Virginia, Edgar Warfield.[394]

Despite the paroles, some of the Southern soldiers remaining behind in Shepherdstown sought to make their way farther south for continued fear of physical capture by the Federals (the Federals did capture Alexander Tinsley in January 1863).[395] Others proved fortunate enough to evade capture. Brothers Jack and Thomas Barlow, the former having been wounded at Sharpsburg, remained in Shepherdstown until late October 1862 after taking up temporary residence at Bedford. The two had already been paroled during the Federal cavalry excursion into town on September 25.[396] However, they decided to take matters into their own hands. The unwounded Thomas hired a wagon driver in Shepherdstown at the steep price of $100 in order to get his brother to the more permanent hospitals in Virginia's interior.[397] Their time in Shepherdstown now over, it was an experience the Barlows would long remember, as many of their comrades never left the small town along the Potomac.

Quartermaster Sergeant Thomas J. Barlow, Thirty-second Virginia Infantry. *Private collection.*

Unfortunately, for all the survival stories that can be found in this tale, one cannot ignore the more than one hundred Confederates who perished in Shepherdstown. Henrietta Bedinger Lee, matron of Bedford, remembered well one such victim. While his comrades escaped to safer havens, Lieutenant Robert Willis of the Thirty-second Virginia lingered in Shepherdstown, having developed typhoid fever following his wounding.[398] On October 3, Willis breathed his last. "I am thankful he is released from pain and grief,"

Lieutenant Robert Willis, Thirty-second Virginia Infantry. *Library of Congress.*

Henrietta Lee wrote. "I believe he was a true Christian, as many of the others were," she finished.[399] Together, Tom Barlow, Mrs. Lee, her daughter Netta, and "a negro boy" buried the young lieutenant in the yard of Bedford.[400] Later, Willis's remains were interred in a more permanent resting place alongside his comrades from the South.

Another Southerner who never left Shepherdstown and never made it to his family was Henry A. Cook of the Thirty-first Georgia Infantry, wounded in the foot at Sharpsburg. While recovering near Shepherdstown, Cook came under the care of blue-clad surgeons, who, deeming it necessary, amputated the mangled foot. During the limb's amputation, Cook expired and left a wife and four children alone on this earth to mourn his loss. Cook's youngest son, Henry Jr., never knew his father. When the war ended, Henry Jr. queried of the returning men, "Are you my papa?" The soldiers, upon learning of the boy's name, found themselves at a loss for words to tell Henry Jr. of the fate his father met in Shepherdstown.[101]

While some Southern families were unable to bring their sons, brothers or fathers back home, others did find the means to do so. Perhaps the most poignant story to come from Shepherdstown's ordeal is that of the boy who served on Nathan Evans's staff—Farquhar Trezevant. Following the loss of his leg, Trezevant began to grow "delirious" as he "[suffered] greatly." At one point, he even believed one of the girls who nursed him was his sister. He asked for a kiss in his delirium and grew troubled when she did not initially comply. After seeing his distress, she kissed the young boy, "but it would not do," wrote Sarah Page Andrews. This incident occurred on September 22, but Trezevant clung to life for another two days. Sarah Andrews sadly reported on September 28, "The poor youth was buried yesterday."[102] At some point following his death, Trezevant's family reinterred his remains in the family plot at Trinity Episcopal Cathedral Cemetery in his hometown of Columbia, South Carolina, following the care he received from the pastor of Shepherdstown's Trinity Episcopal Church.[103]

In September 1862, Shepherdstown had experienced more death than it might have ever cared to see. However, amid the death and destruction, its citizens tried to draw as many positives out of the situation as they could. "[O]h what a mercy to be spared the sorrow of so many Mothers," thought Sarah Andrews.[104] Henrietta Bedinger Lee wrote, "What a season for reflection and self examination this mortality should bring." She began by musing over "how many desolate homes, orphan children and widowed mothers has this vile cruel oppressive war caused[?]"[105] Despite its harrowing experiences, perhaps Shepherdstown could count its blessings, though, that most of its native sons had escaped the bloodiest day in American history, but for whatever that was worth, the "terrible reality and earnestness of war" dropped suddenly on its doorstep in September 1862.[106]

9
"THEIR DEEDS ARE NOT FORGOTTEN"

As elements of the Army of Northern Virginia entered Shepherdstown in June 1863, their entrance stood in stark contrast to the one nine months earlier. This time, the healthy men preceded the stragglers and the ambulances were not filled with the wounded and dying. One participant in this more lively march noted the Confederates "gaily…marched through the streets of Shepherdstown, whose fair daughters greeted us with gladsome smiles, waving their handkerchiefs, and bidding us remember them in the coming struggle."[107] However much the residents of Shepherdstown tried to look ahead, though, events of the past loomed large in their minds.

While the women of Shepherdstown bid adieu to the boys in gray, it is unimaginable that the Confederate soldiers passing through also did not turn their minds to September 1862, when the town's citizens "were devoted in their attention to the wounded and the young ladies angelic in their ministering."[108] The gruesome spectacle that Shepherdstown became in September 1862 was an experience shared by surgeon, soldier and civilian alike and remained an experience not easily erased from one's mind.

Lafayette Guild's Confederate medical corps particularly experienced a trying hour during and following the Maryland Campaign. Lack of transportation and medical supplies, a large disparity between the number of surgeons and wounded men and the recurring problem of straggling all hampered Guild's efforts to effectively remove and treat all of the Army of Northern Virginia's wounded. Guild unfortunately never published an after-action report of the campaign, but in a letter to Samuel Moore dated October

9, 1862, these problems can be easily discerned. "We are in great need of ambulance wagons," Guild bluntly stated. "Our limited transportation has compelled us to leave many wounded in exposed positions, and they have fallen into the hands of the enemy," he continued. Guild further wrote, "While in Maryland we were unable to procure medical supplies to any amount."[109] Clearly, these unavoidable shortcomings made the plight of the wounded Southerner worse than it could have been.

Transportation was not the only essential element of a medical corps lacking in the Army of Northern Virginia. Surgeons, nurses and the like all found themselves vastly outnumbered by the scores of wounded men. Youthful Dr. John Shaffner of the Thirty-third North Carolina Infantry perfectly described the plight of the medical corps during the campaign. "The labors have been too onerous for one man. I have had nearly every operation to perform in the Brigade, throughout the whole campaign." Shaffner admitted in the same letter, "On several occasions I have been nearly compelled to succumb…but *pride* & *sense of duty* have kept me thus constantly at work."[110] Despite the driven soul of a surgeon to continue his work in the face of such odds, Shaffner's pride and sense of duty could not account for the disproportionate amount of wounded he and other Southern surgeons had to treat in the course of September 1862.

Though the Confederate medical corps had traveled leaps and bounds since its establishment in early 1861, problems still plagued it, particularly in officially regulating members of a medical corps and, as mentioned above, removing wounded from the battlefield. In General Orders No. 94, Robert E. Lee expressly laid out who could and could not aid wounded on the battlefield (see Chapter 1). However, when the bullets and shells began to fly, more men than those authorized left the ranks to bring their wounded comrades to safety, thus lessening the number of soldiers on the firing line.[111] The structure of Guild's medical system had not yet caught up with this plaguing problem by the time the Confederate army splashed into Maryland in early September.

Clearly, the surgeons of the Army of Northern Virginia were severely hampered by the shortcomings of its system and its supplies. After contemplating another invasion in the wake of the army's retreat from Maryland, Franklin Gaillard of the Second South Carolina wrote, "It is simply ridiculous to talk of invading with such an army of stragglers as we have and straggling can not [*sic*] be avoided unless the Government has it in its power to put its Quartermaster, Commissary and Medical Department in better condition. This it can not [*sic*] do, cut off as it is from the world and with undeveloped manufacturing resources."[112] Despite the deficiencies, the performance of the Confederate medical corps in the Maryland Campaign was about as good as conditions permitted. Following the campaign, the medical corps aided in rejuvenating the army, helping to double its strength by returning wounded men to the ranks between September 22 and November 11, 1862.[113]

For the Confederate soldier in general—and the wounded Southerner in particular—the Maryland Campaign was one of the toughest they had to endure. Poorly clad and shod on a minimal diet, the Confederacy called upon these decrepit soldiers to achieve its independence.[114] The rough condition of the soldiers did not prevent them from holding onto fond memories of the campaign, however. Perhaps their fondest memories came from the care and reception they received in Shepherdstown.

Scores of contemporaneous accounts written during and after the war by soldiers who passed through Shepherdstown attest to the reception that the men, women and children of the town gave them. Writing from the town, one Southerner remarked, "Everybody is extolling the persevering and tender care nursing of the wounded bestowed by the people of this place."[115] In particular, the women of the town received extra praise. A Virginian recalled of their care:

> *The ladies of Shepherdstown were out in the street with buckets of coffee and biscuits that they would hand the troops as they passed along. They also dressed the wounds of those able to walk. One man in my company was shot in the hand, and a lot of girls dressed his wound. He said it made him feel good to have those girls dressing his wound. It reminded him of a snowbird hopping over an ash bank.*[116]

The kindness and generosity of the people of Shepherdstown ensured that it was a time of relative peace amid a grueling war, something that the Confederates who received such memorable care would never forget.

When the thousands of Confederate wounded came to Shepherdstown and left behind over one hundred dead, the futures of many Southern families came to an abrupt stop. Those who survived the ordeal realized what the residents of Shepherdstown had helped them obtain—a second chance on life. For that, these soldiers would be ever grateful. One of the more common ways soldiers thanked and remembered the citizens of Shepherdstown for their service was to name a newborn child after their caretakers. While receiving aid at the hands of Shepherdstonian Ella Harper, Wyatt Aiken received word of the birth of a daughter on September 20, 1862. In honor of Miss Harper, Aiken and his wife named the baby girl Emma Harper Aiken, getting the first name from his wife's sister.[117] Aiken was not the only soldier to bestow such an honor upon one of his nurses. For the care he received from Netta Lee, Jack Barlow named his daughter Netta.[118]

The memory of the caring residents of Shepherdstown did not fade as the old, gray veterans passed away. On May 31, 1918, Mrs. Bettie Rentch and Miss Annie Licklider received an unexpected guest from a couple on a "peculiar errand." Mr. W.G. Smith of Columbia, South Carolina, was only a boy when his father, Henry J. Smith of the Hampton Legion, died in Shepherdstown of a wound received at Antietam. Upon Henry's death, the patriarch of the Licklider family, whose home Smith died in, sent Smith's widow his "sword and sash and certain other possessions," which spawned a relationship between Smith's widow and Mr. Licklider until both passed away. W.G. Smith "has always had the desire to visit Shepherdstown and his father's grave and to thank those who ministered to the soldiers, or their descendants." In his visit, Mr. Smith found what he desired. Rentch and Licklider told him of his father's stay before taking the younger Smith to his father's grave in Elmwood Cemetery, where most of the Confederates who died in Shepherdstown were buried. Mr. Smith "expressed great appreciation of the kindness of those who had kept it [H.J. Smith's grave] green all these years."[119] In doing so, the citizens of Shepherdstown likewise ensured that they would never forget the events that engulfed their town in September 1862.

The events of September 1862 were not something that Shepherdstonians could simply wipe from their memories. Physical reminders of the harrowing events witnessed by Shepherdstown's citizens scarred the landscape and the town's homes, churches and workplaces for years to come. The pews of St. Peter's Lutheran Church remained bloodstained years after the war.[120] Local homes also found themselves in the paths of the armies. Reverend Robert Douglas, living in Ferry Hill across the Potomac from Shepherdstown, wrote Fitz John Porter in October 1862 describing the damage done to his property since the war's beginning. "My barn was burned down last winter and now the Army is cutting down my timber so that I will have nothing left to rebuild my barn or reconstruct my fences," Douglas complained. He also told Porter of the destruction of several of his outbuildings and almost all of his fences.[121] Surely, the situation across the river could not have been different.

For residents like Dr. John Quigley, the events that transpired in his home in 1862 could not be washed away or built over. When the Army of

Northern Virginia brought its wounded to Shepherdstown, it also brought the disease, vermin and grime that accompanied Civil War armies. The soldiers were not the only ones affected by these scourges of nineteenth-century America. Some Shepherdstonians contracted the diseases brought to their town, and some paid dearly for their roles in aiding the wounded. Quigley's young daughter Julia was one such victim. While ministering to the wounded in her home, Julia Quigley contracted scarlet fever as well as a disease of the throat. "Her sufferings were harrowing," recalled her bereaved father. On October 4, 1862, young Julia died of her diseases. Dr. Quigley wrote in his journal, "I hope I may…be spared to witness such another death, either in my own family, or in any other."[122] Unfortunately, Quigley did witness more death, and for the rest of his life, reminders of that death remained in Shepherdstown.

As Shepherdstonians began to rebuild their fences, repair their homes and attempt to erase the bloody reminders of their fiery trial in September 1862, tangible evidence remained. Of course, as already mentioned, not all of the wounded Southerners hospitalized in Shepherdstown survived their wounds. Most of those who did not were taken to the farm of Jacob Line south of town and buried in what Henrietta Bedinger Lee called "the new Stranger's grave yard."[123] At the end of the war, the *Shepherdstown Register*, which had ceased printing during the war years, called the Confederate graves in the town "a sacred spot" that were "neatly sodded and distinctly marked."[124] The newspaper's editors called on all Shepherdstonians—and anyone else reading the column—to put aside the enmity felt from the war, drop the rifle and pick up the olive branch to restore the nation. "The wooden legs and empty sleeves of gallant soldiers ought to rebuke all vindictive feeling," it concluded.[125]

For all of the talks regarding peace and restoration in the United States following the war, Shepherdstown still flaunted its Southern leanings and continued to remember its most harrowing experience during the war: its time as a Confederate hospital. In 1867, the town's residents organized the Southern Soldiers' Memorial Association, which purchased the lot encompassing many of the Confederate graves in town the following year. The Confederate Cemetery within the larger Elmwood Cemetery was dedicated the next year.[126] Headboards—likely made of wood—adorned each of the one hundred or more graves within the cemetery. However, shortly after its founding, the residents of town sought a more permanent and fitting memorial to commemorate the Confederate dead from across the South buried in their backyard.

Confederate section of Elmwood Cemetery. Many of the Confederate dead buried here perished while being treated in Shepherdstown's buildings following the Maryland Campaign. *Author's collection.*

On June 6, 1870, a crowd of 3,500 people gathered at Elmwood Cemetery for the dedication of a monument to the Confederate dead buried there.[127] The monument called the men lying in its shadow "true patriots" whose "deeds are not forgotten."[128] Joseph McMurran, himself a Confederate veteran, spoke at the dedication. "It is one of the noblest instincts of our nature that leads us to honor the good and brave," he said. McMurran proceeded to call the newly revealed monument "the first of [its] kind" in the Shenandoah Valley and thought it appropriate that it should stand on the Potomac's south shore as "a way mark to inform travelers that they are entering the southland."[129] Indeed, one look at the 162 wooden markers within the cemetery would have left an impression on any passerby of what this town, and its southern brethren, had gone through during the Civil War.[130]

Every June for years after the war, Shepherdstonians young and old returned to the Confederate cemetery to adorn the graves with flowers and to honor the Confederacy. Shepherdstown's experiences in September 1862

Memorial to Confederate dead, Elmwood Cemetery, Shepherdstown. *Photographs of Civil War battlefields and cemeteries in Virginia, Maryland and West Virginia. MSS 12529. Special Collections, University of Virginia, Charlottesville, Virginia.*

were not easily forgotten. In 1884, marble headstones were placed at the head of each grave, giving residents of the past, present and future the most permanent reminder they ever had regarding the ordeal Shepherdstown endured. There was no ignoring those 114 headstones, each one having a story to tell. Shepherdstonians could not escape the carnage and death the town witnessed no matter how far removed they were. For the town, though, it remained an important piece of its history and one that should be told, remembered and, most importantly, written down. "As long as written accounts are preserved, this integral part of our beloved town's heritage [the adornment of the graves] will be remembered," noted one resident, as would the town's trial in 1862.[131] Indeed, how could the town and the soldiers and the surgeons forget it? After all, the week that encompassed the battles at Harpers Ferry, South Mountain, Antietam and Shepherdstown was, in the words of Mary Bedinger Mitchell, "the most trying and tempestuous week of the war for Shepherdstown."[132]

NOTES

Introduction

1. Samuel J.B.V. Gilpin Diary, September 20, 1862, E.N. Gilpin Papers, Library of Congress Manuscript Division (hereafter LOCMD).
2. "A Vast Hospital," *Herald of Freedom and Torch Light*, September 24, 1862, http://www.whilbr.org/itemDetail.aspx?idEntry=753 (accessed December 11, 2014), is the article often cited with giving this name to Sharpsburg and its environs. However, as noted, Gilpin refers to Shepherdstown and the area around it as "one vast Hospital" four days before the *Herald*.
3. Mary Bedinger Mitchell, "A Woman's Recollections of Antietam," in Johnson and Buel, *Battles and Leaders*, 2:690 (hereafter *B&L*).

Chapter 1

4. *New York Times*, "Brady's Photographs: Pictures of the Dead at Antietam," October 20, 1862, 5.
5. Ibid.
6. Chalmers, "Lieutenant-General N.B. Forrest," 454.
7. Cunningham, *Field Services*, 23.
8. Cunningham, *Doctors*, 21; Freemon, *Gangrene*, 29.
9. Freemon, *Gangrene*, 29.

10. Cunningham, *Field Services*, 26.
11. Rafuse, *Single Grand Victory*, 201–04.
12. Blackford and Blackford, *Letters*, 35–36.
13. Freemon, *Gangrene*, 31; Cunningham, *Doctors*, 28; Farr, "Moore," 55.
14. Cunningham, *Field Services*, 69.
15. Farr, "Moore," 45–47; Freemon, *Gangrene*, 31–32.
16. Meier "'No Place for the Sick,'" 189.
17. Sears, *Gates*, 82.
18. Cunningham, *Field Services*, 73–75.
19. Sears, *Gates*, 146–47.
20. Boulware, Diary, May 31, 1862, accession 22042, Personal papers collection, Library of Virginia, Richmond, VA, 23219 (hereafter LVA).
21. Cunningham, *Field Services*, 77–78.
22. Constance Carry Harrison, "Richmond Scenes in '62," *B&L*, 2:443.
23. Sears, *Gates*, 138–40, 145.
24. U.S. War Department, *War of the Rebellion*, ser. 1, vol. 11, pt. 3, 572 (hereafter *OR*; citations are to series 1 unless otherwise stated).
25. Lafayette Guild Compiled Service Record, roll 0113, M 331, Compiled service records of Confederate officers and enlisted men who did not belong to any particular regiment, separate company or comparable unit, or special corps, War Department Collection of Confederate Records, Record Group 109, National Archives Building, Washington, D.C. (hereafter RG 109).
26. Mildred Lewis Rutherford, Surgeon Biographies, Historical Records of the United Daughters of the Confederacy, vol. 20, 137, Medical/Hospital Collection, Eleanor S. Brockenbrough Archives, Museum of the Confederacy (hereafter MOC); Freemon, *Gangrene*, 27, 73.
27. *OR*, vol. 11, pt. 3, 633–34.
28. Ibid., pt. 2, 501–02; Lafayette Guild to A.H. Cole, April 11, 1863, ch. 6, vol. 641, pg. 118, Letters Sent, June 28, 1862–August 29, 1863, Medical Director's Office, Army of Northern Virginia, RG 109.
29. *OR*, vol. 12, pt. 3, 928.
30. See Black, *Surgeon*, 38, for example of lack of surgeons, when he and one assistant had to care for 225 men following Second Manassas; Hartwig, *Antietam Creek*, 67.
31. Cunningham, *Field Services*, 83–84.
32. Ibid., 88–90.
33. Duncan, *Medical Department*, 32.
34. Black, *Surgeon*, 38.

35. *OR* vol. 19, pt. 2, 606.
36. Lafayette Guild to Samuel P. Moore, September 6, 1862, ch. 6, vol. 641, pg. 9, Letters Sent, June 28, 1862–August 29, 1863, Medical Director's Office, Army of Northern Virginia, RG 109.
37. Hood, *Advance and Retreat*, 38; Harsh, *Taken at the Flood*, 68–69.
38. Lafayette Guild to James C. Herndon, September 7, 1862, ch. 6, vol. 641, pg. 10, Letters Sent, June 28, 1862–August 29, 1863, Medical Director's Office, Army of Northern Virginia, RG 109.
39. Lafayette Guild to Robert H. Chilton, September 9, 1862, ch. 6, vol. 641, pg. 11, Letters Sent, June 28, 1862–August 29, 1863, Medical Director's Office, Army of Northern Virginia, RG 109. For Guild's assessment of Confederate ambulances, see Lafayette Guild to Samuel P. Moore, November 22, 1862, ch. 6, vol. 641, pg. 37, Letters Sent, June 28, 1862–August 29, 1863, Medical Director's Office, Army of Northern Virginia, RG 109.
40. Cunningham, *Field Services*, 91.

Chapter 2

41. Mitchell, "Recollections," *B&L*, 2:686.
42. West Virginia did not officially become a state until June 20, 1863. Therefore, the author will refer to Shepherdstown as a part of Virginia, just as it was in September 1862.
43. Conway, *Shepherdstown*, 4–5.
44. Town founder Thomas Shepherd established a gristmill in Shepherdstown shortly after he arrived there, powered by the Town Run. See Conway, *Shepherdstown*, 6. In addition, in 1788, the Virginia Assembly authorized the opening of a tobacco inspection warehouse along the Potomac River in Shepherdstown. The location was ideal due to its proximity to the river. See Belfoure, "Historic Structures." Lastly, it should be noted that Shepherdstown exists and is located where it is because of its closeness to a ford on the Potomac River, which allowed settlers to cross the river and enter the Shenandoah Valley. See Conway, *Shepherdstown*, 4.
45. Conway, *Shepherdstown*, 16–18.
46. *Shepherdstown Register*, "Census Figures Show Decrease in Population Here," July 28, 1860, reprinted in *Shepherdstown Register*, December 4, 1949, Section C; Virginia Memory, "Map of April 17, 1861, Vote

On Secession," 2014, http://www.virginiamemory.com/docs/hires/april_17_1861_vote.pdf (accessed January 27, 2015).

47. Virginia Memory, "Map, Vote On Secession."

48. Kenamond, *Prominent Men*, 18–20; Charles Wesley Andrews to Matthew Page Andrews, May 17, 1861, Charles Wesley Andrews Papers, David M. Rubenstein Rare Book and Manuscript Library, Duke University (hereafter CWA Papers); Walker, *Memoir*, 130.

49. *Shepherdstown Register*, "The Excitement in Shepherdstown," October 22, 1859.

50. *(Charlestown) Virginia Free Press*, "Report of Col. Robert W. Baylor Commander of Virginia Troops at Harpers Ferry," November 3, 1859.

51. *Shepherdstown Register*, "The Insurrection at Harper's Ferry," November 5, 1859.

52. Ibid., "'Shepherdstown Auxiliary Guards!,'" November 5, 1859.

53. Ibid., "If Black Republican President Is Elected Should South Secede?," January 28, 1860, reprinted in *Shepherdstown Register*, December 4, 1949, Section C.

54. Virginia Memory, "Map, Vote On Secession."

55. Conway, *Shepherdstown*, 23.

56. Douglas, *I Rode with Stonewall*, 6.

57. Musser, *History of Shepherdstown*, 90–91.

58. Mitchell, "Recollections," *B&L*, 2:686–88; Mary Bedinger Mitchell Biography, Historic Shepherdstown Museum.

59. Lee, *Lee of Virginia*, 514–15.

60. Walker, *Biographical Sketches*, 420–21; Scott, *Orange County*, 268–69.

61. Walker, *Biographical Sketches*, 421; Scott, *Orange County*, 269.

62. Shepherdstown lore has placed the relationship between William Parran and the Parran family in Shepherdstown as that of a prodigal son returning home. In fact, William Parran was not the son of the Parrans in Shepherdstown but was the nephew of the matriarch Laura Parran and thus the cousin of Laura's daughter Lillie. The author constructed the Parran family tree having obtained this information from Lee, *Lee of Virginia*, 515; Virginia Military Institute, "VMI Historical Archives Rosters: William Sellman Parran," http://archivesweb.vmi.edu/rosters/record.php?ID=516 (accessed April 5, 2015); Cordell, *Medical Annals*, 528. In addition, see Alexander L. Tinsley to Earl G. Swem, February 6, 1939, Alexander Tinsley Faculty-Alumni File, University Archives Faculty-Alumni File Collection, Special Collections Research Center, Earl Gregg Swem Library, College of William and Mary (hereafter Tinsley Alumni

File), which claims William S. Parran as the cousin of Shepherdstown's Parran family.

63. William S. Parran to Linn, Campbell Family Papers, Special Collections Research Center, Swem Library, College of William and Mary (hereafter Campbell Family Papers).
64. Society of the Lees of Virginia, "Recollections of Netta Lee," 13.
65. Snyder, *John Snyder*, 65.
66. Mitchell, "Recollections," *B&L*, 2:688.
67. CWA to Matthew Page Andrews, September 17, 1862, CWA Papers.

Chapter 3

68. Bartlett, *Military Record of Louisiana*, 143.
69. Wardlaw, Diary, September 18, 1862, Antietam National Battlefield (hereafter ANB); Owen, *In Camp and Battle*, 160.
70. Benson, *Civil War Book*, 26.
71. Lee's plan is well known, but the best explanation can be found in Harsh, *Taken at the Flood*, 84.
72. *OR* vol. 19, pt. 2, 593–94.
73. Army of Northern Virginia General Order No. 102, September 4, 1862, David Addison Weisiger Papers, Virginia Historical Society, Richmond, VA (hereafter VHS); *OR* vol. 19, pt. 2, 641.
74. Harsh, *Sounding the Shallows*, 165.
75. Luvaas and Nelson, *Army War College Guide*, 274.
76. *OR* vol. 19, pt. 2, 590.
77. Steiner, *Report*, 20–21.
78. *OR* vol. 19, pt. 2, 603–04.
79. Caldwell, *History of a Brigade of South Carolinians*, 41.
80. Robert E. Lee to Jeb Stuart, September 12, 1862, 2:30 p.m., James Ewell Brown Stuart Papers, Henry E. Huntington Library, San Marino, CA.
81. Ibid.; *OR* 11, 3:639; Denney, *Civil War Medicine*, 152, states that "a flood of nearly 400 sick Confederates" were brought into Frederick on September 6. It seems reasonable to assume that this is the approximate number Lee left behind in Frederick when he began moving his army west.
82. *OR* vol. 19, pt. 1, 139.
83. Ibid., 107, 110; see George E. Waller to Doctor, September 25, 1862, in the George E. Waller Letters #1512, Southern Historical Collection, Wilson Library, University of North Carolina at Chapel Hill (hereafter

SHC), for reference to the Federals destroying all their medical stores in Frederick prior to the arrival of the Army of Northern Virginia.
84. See Boulware, Diary, September 7–8, 1862, for examples of medical wagons falling behind.
85. Stilwell, *Stilwell Letters*, 61.
86. Black, *Surgeon*, 38.
87. Jedediah Hotchkiss to Sara Anne Comfort Hotchkiss, September 8, 1862, Reel 4, Jedediah Hotchkiss Papers, LOCMD.

Chapter 4

88. Trimpi, "Lafayette McLaws' Aide-de-Camp," 32.
89. Dickert, *Kershaw's Brigade*, 148.
90. Ibid., 164.
91. *OR* vol. 19, pt. 1, 863; Dickert, *Kershaw's Brigade*, 148.
92. Dickert, *Kershaw's Brigade*, 148.
93. *OR* vol. 19, pt. 1, 861.
94. McDaniel, *Diary of Battles*, 12; Hartwig, *Antietam Creek*, 257.
95. Hoptak, *South Mountain*, 42, 53.
96. *OR* vol. 19, pt. 1, 1,041.
97. Jordan and Manarin, *North Carolina Troops*, 446; *Raleigh Spirit of the Age*, "20th N.C.," October 6, 1862.
98. John C. Gorman, "From Our Army: An Account of the Late Battles," *Raleigh Weekly Standard*, October 1, 1862.
99. Cole, *Huntsville to Appomattox*, 241.
100. *OR* vol. 19, pt. 1, 922.
101. Cole, *Huntsville to Appomattox*, 64, 71.
102. Battle, *Third Alabama!*, 55.
103. John K. Hoyt to Robert Alexander Lancaster, September 18, 1862, Robert Alexander Lancaster Papers, VHS; ibid., October 3, 1862, Robert Alexander Lancaster Papers, VHS.
104. *OR* vol. 19, pt. 1, 894.
105. Lucy Cleveland, "Dr. Baruch's Experiences as a Prisoner of War," *New York Times*, December 8, 1912.
106. Ibid.
107. Boulware, Diary, September 14, 1862, LVA.
108. Dooley, *Confederate Soldier*, 34–35. Robert E. Lee in fact, was not wounded. Rather, on August 31, his horse Traveller became startled

while Lee held on to the reins, forcing the general to fall. "Instinctively he broke his fall with his hands and in the process broke a bone in one of them and sprained them both," wrote a biographer of Lee. These injuries to his hands prevented Lee from riding a horse for much of the Maryland Campaign and forced him to ride in the rear of an ambulance. See Thomas, *Robert E. Lee*, 255.

109. Dooley, *Confederate Soldier*, 35.
110. Boulware, Diary, September 14, 1862, LVA.
111. Bernard, *War Talks*, 27.
112. Ibid.
113. Ibid., 304–05.
114. Hoptak, *South Mountain*, 148.
115. Bernard, *War Talks*, 29.
116. *OR* vol. 19, pt. 1, 827.
117. Von Borcke, *Memoirs*, 1:217.
118. *OR* vol. 19, pt. 1, 864.
119. Trimpi, "Lafayette McLaws' Aide-de-Camp," 36.

Chapter 5

120. Mitchell, "Recollections," *B&L*, 2:688.
121. H.L. Snyder, "Notes by Observer," *Shepherdstown Register*, September 22, 1921.
122. Sorrel, *Recollections*, 107–08; Hartwig, *Antietam Creek*, 478.
123. Cole, *From Huntsville to Appomattox*, 64.
124. Cutts, "A.S. Cutts to Dr. J. William Jones," 429–31.
125. Hubbs, *Voices from Company D*, 109.
126. Shotwell, *Papers*, 1:340.
127. Wise, *Seventeenth Virginia Infantry*, 114.
128. Hartwig, *Antietam Creek*, 683–84.
129. Albert, *Forty-Fifth Regiment*, 48.
130. *OR* vol. 19, pt. 1, 376.
131. Reese, *Sealed with Their Lives*, 201.
132. Ibid., 199.
133. *OR* vol. 19, pt. 1, 107.
134. Special Orders No. 194, M921, roll 2, Orders and Circulars Issued by the Army of the Potomac and the Army and Department of Northern Virginia, C.S.A., 1861–1865, RG 109; Steiner, *Report*, 16–17.
135. Weaver and Wallace, *Richmond Ambulance Co.*, 26.

136. John Herbig, "Recruits Wanted for an Infirmary Company," *Richmond Daily Dispatch*, March 22, 1862.
137. Lafayette Guild to James C. Herndon, September 16, 1862, ch. 6, vol. 641, pg. 11, Letters Sent, June 28, 1862–August 29, 1863, Medical Director's Office, Army of Northern Virginia, RG 109.
138. Dooley, *Confederate Soldier*, 38–39.
139. Boulware, Diary, September 11, 1862, LVA.
140. Guild to Moore, November 22, 1862, ch. 6, vol. 641, pg. 36, Letters Sent, June 28, 1862–August 29, 1863, Medical Director's Office, Army of Northern Virginia, RG 109. See also Taylor, *Lee's Adjutant*, 45–46, for an example of a member of Lee's staff having to guess the general's intentions.
141. Dr. John Mutius Gaines Biography, John Nelson Federal Hospitals Project Research Notes, Part 1, Box 1, John H. Nelson Collection, ANB.
142. Cleveland, "Dr. Baruch's Experiences."
143. Ibid. It might seem strange that Baruch then only realized "war is hell" during the second year of the war, but he had not been in the army long before the Maryland Campaign; indeed, Second Manassas was the first battle he participated in.
144. Ibid.
145. G.W.B., "Maryland Campaign: The Cavalry Fight at Boonsboro Graphically Described," *Richmond Dispatch*, July 4, 1897.
146. Cleveland, "Dr. Baruch's Experiences."
147. G.W.B., "Maryland Campaign."
148. Cleveland, "Dr. Baruch's Experiences."
149. Carman, *Maryland Campaign*, 568. For a detailed description of the Ninth's role in the fight at Boonsboro, see McClellan, *I Rode with Jeb Stuart*, 124–25.
150. G.W.B., "Maryland Campaign."
151. McClellan, *I Rode with Jeb Stuart*, 125–26.
152. Douglas, *I Rode with Stonewall*, 168.
153. The Confederate hospitals in Boonsboro have been discussed earlier in Chapter 5. See von Borcke, *Memoirs*, 1:217, for reference to Confederate wounded in Pleasant Valley. Von Borcke does not explicitly mention Confederate hospitals in the valley, but since Lafayette McLaws's command was boxed in on nearly every side on the night of September 14, there would have been no other place for the wounded from the fights at Crampton's Gap and Maryland Heights to go; see *OR* vol. 19, pt. 1, 856, for McLaws's description of his penned-in position on September 14 and 15. See *OR* vol. 19, pt. 1, 857, in which McLaws mentions going

to Charlestown "to look after the sick and wounded from Pleasant Valley." The fact that McLaws's wounded were immediately moved to Charlestown once he removed his command from Pleasant Valley implies that the town was already being used as a hospital prior to the surrender of Harpers Ferry's garrison. Charlestown, Virginia, is modern Charles Town, West Virginia.

154. *OR* vol. 19, pt. 1, 857; Welch, *Confederate Surgeon's Letters*, 31–32. Welch was a surgeon in the Thirteenth South Carolina Infantry, Gregg's Brigade, A.P. Hill's Division. Hill's Division participated in the capture of Harpers Ferry, and Welch's presence in Charlestown is further proof of the Confederate wounded from Harpers Ferry being removed to that location.

155. Harsh, *Taken at the Flood*, 293.

156. Surgeon General's Office Circular, May 7, 1862, ch. 6, vol. 648, pg. 4, Letters Sent and Letters, Orders and Circulars Received, General Hospital No. 1, Savannah, GA, 1862–1864, RG 109.

157. Harsh, *Taken at the Flood*, 301.

158. White, *Richmond Howitzer Battalion*, 132.

159. Neese, *Three Years*, 125.

160. W.T. Field to Ezra A. Carman, March 2, 1895, Antietam Studies, Records of the Adjutant General's Office, Record Group 94, National Archives Building, Washington, D.C. (hereafter NA-AS).

161. Shotwell, *Papers*, 345–46.

162. Society of the Lees of Virginia, "Recollections of Netta Lee," 13.

163. Mitchell, "Recollections," *B&L*, 2:689.

164. Ibid., 688.

165. Ibid., 689. Mitchell wrote of the presence, or lack thereof, of Confederate army surgeons on September 15: "No surgeons were to be seen. A few men, detailed as nurses, had come, but they were incompetent, of course." However, it does not seem realistic that the Confederate wounded simply wandered aimlessly through the western Maryland countryside and were not guided by some direction and were not accompanied by army surgeons.

166. In *OR* vol. 19, pt. 1, 110, medical director of the Army of the Potomac Jonathan Letterman described rides in Civil War ambulance wagons as "tedious and tiresome, and often painful" for those who rode in them. Rides in two-wheeled ambulances were said to have been so bad that "no man who has once ridden in the two-wheeled ambulance would willingly get into one again, even if he were well." Another said of these types of ambulance, "Their motion was intolerable and excruciating [and]

wounded men begged to be taken out." The four-wheeled ambulances, while they were improvements over their two-wheeled predecessors, were still not perfect. Even with spring suspension, soldiers lying on beds inside of them "had to hold on with both hands to keep from falling to the floor." Haller, *Battlefield Medicine*, 46–47.

167. Mitchell, "Recollections," *B&L*, 2:689.
168. Sarah Page Andrews to Page Andrews, September 18, 1862, CWA Papers.
169. Mitchell, "Recollections," *B&L*, 2:689.
170. CWA to Matthew Page Andrews, September 17, 1862, CWA Papers.
171. Mitchell, "Recollections," *B&L*, 2:689.
172. CWA to Matthew Page Andrews, September 17, 1862, CWA Papers.
173. Mitchell, "Recollections," *B&L*, 2:689.
174. Ibid., 690.
175. Society of the Lees of Virginia, "Recollections of Netta Lee," 14–15; Snyder, "Notes," *Shepherdstown Register*, September 22, 1921; Kenamond, *Prominent Men*, 86–87.
176. Mitchell, "Recollections," *B&L*, 2:690.
177. Ibid.
178. Phillip F. Liddell Compiled Service Record, roll 0195, M 269, Compiled service records of Confederate soldiers from Mississippi units, labeled with each soldier's name, rank, and unit, with links to revealing documents about each soldier, RG 109.
179. Stubbs, *Duty, Honor, Valor*, 656–57.
180. Ibid., 300–01.
181. Sarah Page Andrews to Page Andrews, September 18, 1862, CWA Papers; Stubbs, *Duty, Honor, Valor*, 656.
182. Guild to Herndon, September 16, 1862, ch. 6, vol. 641, pg. 11, RG 109.
183. Owen, *In Camp and Battle*, 142.
184. Thomas Clark, "A Soldier's Life," The Letters of Thomas Clark, State Archives of Florida, Florida Department of State.

Chapter 6

185. Monroe, *Battery D*, 13–14.
186. Ibid.
187. Mitchell, "Recollections," *B&L*, 2:690.
188. CWA to Matthew Page Andrews, September 17, 1862, CWA Papers.
189. H.L. Snyder, "Notes by Observer," *Shepherdstown Register*, September 22, 1927.

190. See Gentile, "Hidden, in Plain Sight"; Harsh, *Taken at the Flood*, 345.
191. Zax, "Civil War Geology."
192. Taylor, *De Quibus*, 302, 330.
193. Ibid., 302.
194. At the Battle of Antietam, regimental hospitals would have been found in homes, barns or tents several hundred yards behind the front lines. Some good examples of these would be the Reel Barn and the Piper House, whose roles will be discussed later in this chapter.
195. Blanton, *Medicine in Virginia*, 279.
196. Surgeon General's Office Circular, May 7, 1862, ch. VI, vol. 648, pg. 4, Letters Sent and Letters, Orders, and Circulars Received, General Hospital No. 1, Savannah, GA, 1862–1864, RG 109.
197. Trimpi, "Lafayette McLaws' Aide-de-Camp," 39. The Battle of Malvern Hill, fought on July 1, 1862, outside Richmond, witnessed the superiority of Federal artillery—at least thirty-six guns, to be exact—breaking apart any attacks Confederate infantry made toward them. The effectiveness of the Federal guns caused General D.H. Hill to later remark of the battle: "It was not war—it was murder." See Sears, *Gates*, 291; Daniel H. Hill, "McClellan's Change of Base and Malvern Hill," in *B&L*, 2:394.
198. Boulware, Diary, September 17, 1862, LVA.
199. Autobiographical essay by Francis Marion Parker, in the Francis M. Parker Papers #4896, SHC.
200. Hood, *Advance and Retreat*, 44.
201. Carman, *Maryland Campaign*, vol. 2, *Antietam*, 59.
202. Ibid.
203. Bradwell, *Under the Southern Cross*, 90.
204. Ibid.; White, *31st Georgia Volunteer Infantry*, 51.
205. *Atlanta Southern Confederacy*, October 8, 1862, copy in Thirteenth Georgia Volunteer Infantry Regiment file, ANB.
206. Judson A. Butts, *Monroe (GA) Advertiser*, September 17, 1889, quoted in White, *31st Georgia Volunteer Infantry*, 51–53.
207. Eicher and Eicher, *Civil War High Commands*, 341–42.
208. Alexander, *Fighting for the Confederacy*, 154.
209. Douglas, *I Rode with Stonewall*, 169–70.
210. *Savannah (GA) Daily Morning News*, "The Thirteenth Georgia in the Battle of Sharpsburg," October 4, 1862, copy in Thirteenth Georgia file, ANB.
211. Holsworth, "Uncommon Valor," 18.
212. Sturkey, *Hampton Legion Infantry C.S.A.*, 305.

213. Welch, *Welch*, 3:6.
214. Carman, *Maryland Campaign*, vol. 2, *Antietam*, 90.
215. *OR* vol. 19, pt. 1, 931.
216. Henry J. Smith Compiled Service Record, roll 0370, M 267, Compiled service records of Confederate soldiers from South Carolina units, RG 109.
217. *OR* vol. 19, pt. 1, 931.
218. Welch, *Welch*, 8.
219. Todd, *First Texas Regiment*, 11.
220. Welch, *Welch*, 8.
221. Harsh, *Taken at the Flood*, 373.
222. Snyder, "Notes"; Hotchkiss, *Make Me a Map*, 82.
223. Neese, *Three Years*, 125.
224. Snyder, "Notes." See Carman, *Maryland Campaign*, 152, for information on Confederate cavalry deployed to prevent stragglers from going to the rear.
225. Atkinson, Memoir, Ms1994-022, Special Collections, Virginia Polytechnic Institute and State University, Blacksburg, VA.
226. Mitchell, "Recollections," *B&L*, 2:691.
227. Krick, *Lee's Colonels*, 118; Hewett, Trudeau and Suderow, *Supplement to the Official Records of the Union and Confederate Armies*, 3:587 (hereafter cited as *SOR*).
228. DeRosset, "Additional Sketch Third Regiment," 1:226.
229. Carman, *Maryland Campaign*, 122–23.
230. William L. DeRosset Compiled Service Record, roll 0125, M 270, Compiled service records of Confederate soldiers from North Carolina units, RG 109.
231. See Betts, *Experience of a Confederate Chaplain*, 20, for a discussion of DeRosset's immobile nature following his wound.
232. Thomas, *Doles-Cook Brigade*, 82–83.
233. *OR* vol. 19, pt. 1, 1,043–44.
234. Snyder, "Notes."
235. Jensen, *32nd Virginia Infantry*, 90.
236. *OR* vol. 19, pt. 1, 858.
237. McDaniel, *Diary of Battles*, 15.
238. Ibid., 15–16.
239. *OR* vol. 19, pt. 1, 865; McDaniel, *Diary of Battles*, 16.
240. H.W. Addison to Ezra A. Carman, July 4, 1898, NA-AS.
241. McDaniel, *Diary of Battles*, 16.
242. Ibid.; Addison to Carman, July 4, 1898, NA-AS.
243. Pritchard, *Colonel D. Wyatt Aiken*, 2.
244. Addison to Carman, July 4, 1898, NA-AS.
245. Jensen, *32nd Virginia*, 91–94.

246. Ibid., 173–74; Society of the Lees of Virginia, "Recollections of Netta Lee," 14; Civil War Service, Notes of Annie Cox Barlow, private collection; Eicher and Eicher, *Civil War High Commands*, 343.
247. Autobiographical essay, Francis M. Parker Papers, SHC.
248. Eicher and Eicher, *Civil War High Commands*, 104.
249. Seaton Gales, "Sketch of Gen. Geo. B. Anderson," *Our Living and Our Dead (New Bern, NC)*, November 12, 1873.
250. Gorman, "From Our Army."
251. Lee, *Forget-Me-Nots*, 76.
252. Gales, "Sketch."
253. Gorman, "From Our Army."
254. Waters and Edmonds, *Small but Spartan Band*, 35–37.
255. Ellie Reutch to Martha Ann Clark, November 14, 1862, Clark Letters, State Archives of Florida.
256. Bird Wright to Amy Wright, September 21, 1862, Civil War Papers 1862–1865, Special Collections, Robert Manning Strozier Library, Florida State University, Tallahassee, FL (hereafter FSU).
257. Gorman, "From Our Army."
258. Gales, "Sketch."
259. Gorman, "From Our Army."
260. Gales, "Sketch."
261. Lee, *Forget-Me-Nots*, 77.
262. Stone, *Wandering to Glory*, 91.
263. Ibid., 6.
264. Ibid., 67; Silverman, Thomas and Evans, *Shanks*, 115–16.
265. Stone, *Wandering to Glory*, 67–68; Silverman, Thomas and Evans, *Shanks*, 115.
266. In fact, thirteen-year-old Charlie King, a drummer boy in the Forty-ninth Pennsylvania, is often regarded as the youngest casualty of the battle and one of the youngest in the entire war. He, like Trezevant, was mortally wounded by an artillery projectile. See National Park Service, "Antietam: People and Places."
267. Hunter, *Johnny Reb and Billy Yank*, 290–91.
268. Unpublished report of Lieutenant Richard Graves, Wise Artillery, NA-AS. It is unclear just how Dr. Parran ended up fighting with the Wise Artillery. Parran's undated letter to his wife, written "10 miles from Hagerstown," explains that he was still with the Maryland batteries serving in A.R. Courtney's Artillery Battalion, Lawton's Division. Parran goes on to explain, "When Capt. [William] Crenshaw [commanding a battery in A.P. Hill's Division] heard that there would be a change in our [battalion]

he said if I lost my situation, he would like to secure my services for them." One scenario is that Parran briefly joined Crenshaw's Battery and marched with or just ahead of it or other elements of A.P. Hill's Division on their march to Sharpsburg, where Parran stumbled upon the Wise Artillery and volunteered to assist in loading and firing the guns. William S. Parran to Jennie Graves Parran, undated, Campbell Family Papers.

269. William C. Scott to Pamelia Graves Scott, September 19, 1862, Campbell Family Papers; William C. Scott to Pamelia Graves Scott, September 19, 1862, Campbell Family Papers. The two letters dated September 19 detail the death of William S. Parran. Their author, William C. Scott, served with Crenshaw's Battery. His wife and William Parran's wife were likely sisters, making Scott and Parran brothers-in-law.

270. Hunter, *Johnny Reb and Billy Yank*, 291–93.

271. Warfield, *Manassas to Appomattox*, 102.

272. Trimpi, "Lafayette McLaws' Aide-de-Camp," 40.

273. John G. Walker, "Sharpsburg," in *B&L*, 2:681.

274. Jensen, *32nd Virginia*, 95–96.

275. Boulware, Diary, September 17, 1862, LVA.

276. Sorrel, *Recollections*, 118.

277. Sharpsburg Hospitals List, John Nelson Federal Hospitals Project Research Notes, Part 2, John H. Nelson Collection, ANB.

278. "Mount Airy Has Its Moment of History," Steven Grove Farm, Mt. Airy Folder, John Nelson Federal Hospitals Project Research Notes, Part 2, John H. Nelson Collection, ANB.

279. *Charleston Mercury*, "The Battle of Sharpsburg," October 2, 1862.

280. Ibid., "The Battle of Sharpsburg and the Retreat of Our Army Into Virginia," October 3, 1862; Nisbet, *Four Years*, 111.

281. Hotchkiss, *Make Me a Map*, 83; Shaw, *Stonewall Jackson's Surgeon*, 24.

282. Harsh, *Sounding the Shallows*, 201.

283. Andrews, *Footprints of a Regiment*, 88, 203.

284. *OR* vol. 19, pt. 1, 842.

285. Addison to Carman, July 4, 1898, NA-AS.

286. Reilly, *Battlefield of Antietam*.

Chapter 7

287. Mitchell, "Recollections," *B&L*, 2:691.

288. Snyder, "Notes."

289. Mitchell, "Recollections," *B&L*, 2:691.
290. Snyder, "Notes."
291. *Shepherdstown Register*, July 28, 1921.
292. Snyder, "Notes."
293. Sarah Page Andrews to Page Andrews, September 18, 1862, CWA Papers.
294. Carman, *Maryland Campaign*, 611.
295. Holloway, Diary, 4th Texas Infantry, 31–32, Transcription in Diary Collection, MOC.
296. Trimpi, "Lafayette McLaws' Aide-de-Camp," 40.
297. Dinkins, *1861 to 1865*, 62–63.
298. Pritchard, *Colonel D. Wyatt Aiken*, 3–4.
299. Snyder, "Notes."
300. Alexander, *Fighting for the Confederacy*, 146.
301. *Charleston Mercury*, "Correspondence of the Savannah Republican," October 3, 1862.
302. Moore, *Story of a Cannoneer*, 156–57.
303. Lee, *William Nelson Pendleton*, 217; Dickert, *Kershaw's Brigade*, 160; Caldwell, *History of a Brigade of South Carolinians*, 49, points to "the scarcity of ambulances and the rapidity of the withdrawal of the army" as the primary reasons wounded soldiers had to be left behind.
304. *OR* vol. 19, pt. 1, 111.
305. Ibid., 972.
306. Salisbury Watchman, "From the Raleigh Standard—6th N.C. Reg't, Sept. 17th, 1862.," *Fayetteville (NC) Semi-Weekly Observer*, October 2, 1862; Black, *Surgeon*, 38, mentions surgeons "cast[ing] lots" to determine who remained behind with the wounded once an army moved from the battlefield.
307. Dickert, *Kershaw's Brigade*, 160.
308. Shotwell, *Papers*, 358.
309. Von Borcke, *Memoirs*, 1:240.
310. Shotwell, *Papers*, 357.
311. *Charleston Mercury*, "Savannah Republican," October 3, 1862.
312. Wardlaw, Diary, September 18, 1862, ANB.
313. Trimpi, "Lafayette McLaws' Aide-de-Camp," 42; Von Borcke, *Memoirs*, 1:241.
314. Bartlett, *Military Record of Louisiana*, 140.
315. Ibid., 143.
316. Betts, *Experience of a Confederate Chaplain*, 18.
317. Owen, *In Camp and Battle*, 160.
318. Warfield, *Memoirs*, 102.

319. McClellan, *I Rode with Jeb Stuart*, 133.
320. Turner, *Civil War Letters*, 54.
321. Owen, *In Camp and Battle*, 162.
322. Mitchell, "Recollections," *B&L*, 2:691.
323. Snyder, "Notes."
324. Society of the Lees of Virginia, "Recollections of Netta Lee," 14.
325. Mitchell, "Recollections," *B&L*, 2:691.
326. *See Shepherd's Town*, 3:117.
327. Sarah Page Andrews to Page Andrews, September 18, 1862, CWA Papers.
328. CWA to Matthew Page Andrews, September 17, 1862, CWA Papers.
329. Sarah Page Andrews to Page Andrews, September 18, 1862, CWA Papers.
330. Snyder, "Notes."
331. Kenamond, *Prominent Men*, 88–90.
332. *Shepherdstown Register*, "Grant's Pump," July 31, 1924.
333. Shotwell, *Papers*, 362.
334. Henrietta Bedinger Lee to Ida Rust, October 3, 1862, Goldsborough Family Papers, Scarborough Library, Shepherd University.
335. Tinsley to Swem, February 6, 1939, Tinsley Alumni File, W&M.
336. Mitchell, "Recollections," *B&L*, 2:692.
337. Ibid., 694.
338. Snyder, "Notes."
339. Mitchell, "Recollections," *B&L*, 2:692.
340. Ibid., 692–93.
341. Gales, "Sketch."
342. Margie Boteler to Mrs. Anderson, September 18, 1862, from November 30, 1996 auction catalogue of Signature House, Monkton, MD.
343. Gales, "Sketch."
344. *North Carolina Standard*, "Death of Gen. George B. Anderson," October 17, 1862.
345. *Rockingham (Harrisonburg, VA) Register*, "Our Wounded Soldiers," September 26, 1862.
346. Lee, *Civil War Journal*, 143.
347. Clayton G. Coleman to Lucy Coleman, September 27, 1862, Clayton G. Coleman Papers, Virginia Military Institute Archives.
348. *OR* vol. 19, pt. 2, 615.
349. Snyder, "Notes"; Courtney Bird Jones to S.W.P. Andrews, September 22, 1862, CWA Papers.
350. William C. Scott to Pamelia Graves Scott, September 19, 1862, Campbell Family Papers.

351. Tinsley to Swem, February 6, 1939, Tinsley Alumni File, W&M.
352. Walker, *Biographical Sketches*, 421.
353. William S. Parran to Jennie Graves Parran, undated, Campbell Family Papers.
354. This author could not find any Confederate records regarding the number of soldiers treated in Shepherdstown. It is likely that none exist, as Confederate surgeons originally viewed Shepherdstown as a field hospital. Usually, only general hospitals kept detailed records of the names and numbers of patients who were treated. Shepherdstown did become a general hospital following the evacuation of the wounded on September 19, as most of those who stayed, or were left behind, remained in town for weeks or months following the conclusion of the Maryland Campaign. The author arrived at the number of approximately six thousand Confederates treated in Shepherdstown during its brief stint as a field hospital through careful studies of the number of Confederates wounded in all of the battles of the Maryland Campaign while taking into account those wounded who were captured by the Federals as well as those preliminarily treated in Charlestown and other points in the Shenandoah Valley before their removal to the general hospitals at Winchester and other points in the Valley.
355. Sarah Page Andrews to Page Andrews, September 18, 1862, CWA Papers.

Chapter 8

356. *OR* vol. 11, pt. 1, 742. While Porter may have had a reputation in the South for firing on Southern hospitals, in the smoke and dust of battle, it seems likely that whatever troops did fire on a hospital—purposefully or not—they could not have realized it. In this case, it is more likely that Pleasonton's shells landed among Shepherdstown's more populated areas, as he was the first Federal officer on the scene. By the time Porter and his guns arrived, most of the Confederate forces beyond Shepherdstown that Pleasonton's gunners were likely trying to hit before their aim fell short would have been out of the direct vicinity of Shepherdstown.
357. Ibid., vol. 19, pt. 1, 339.
358. Ibid., 831, 151.
359. Mason, *Popular Life*, 151. In reality, Pendleton only lost four guns.
360. James Keith Boswell to Alfred Landon Rives, September 29, 1862, Rives Family Papers, VHS.

361. *OR* vol. 19, pt. 1, 340.
362. Wardlaw, Diary, September 20, 1862, ANB.
363. *New York Times*, "Latest Reports from Headquarters," September 22, 1862.
364. A.J. Dula, "Civil War Incidents as Told by an Old Veteran from Memory," Twenty-second North Carolina Folder, Gettysburg National Military Park (hereafter GNMP).
365. John Francis Shaffner Address, 1903, Fries and Shaffner Family Papers, #4046, SHC.
366. Mitchell, "Recollections," *B&L*, 2:694.
367. Snyder, "Notes."
368. "Notes of Surgical Cases, Battle of Shepherdstown or Butler's [*sic*] Ford on the 20th Septr. 1862," J.W. Powell Surgical Notebook, January 1862–September 1864, Box 1, Medical and Hospital Series, Medical Personnel Collection, MOC.
369. *New York Times*, "From Sharpsburgh," October 22, 1862.
370. Ellie Reutch to Martha Ann Clark, November 14, 1862, Clark Letters, State Archives of Florida.
371. Bird Wright to Amy Wright, September 21, 1862, Civil War Papers 1862–1865, Special Collections, FSU.
372. B.B. Wright Compiled Service Record, roll 0086, M 251, Compiled service records of Confederate soldiers from Florida units, RG 109.
373. Snyder, "Notes"; Betts, *Experience of a Confederate Chaplain*, 20. The *Shepherdstown Register* article cited above recalls Atwell being a native of Georgia. This article, however, was written secondhand nearly sixty years after the events discussed. Numerous contemporary sources speak of a Captain Atwell from North Carolina who was mortally wounded at Sharpsburg and died in Shepherdstown, leading the author to believe that the Georgian Atwell is really the Atwell from North Carolina.
374. *New York Times*, "From Sharpsburgh."
375. Lafayette Guild to Thomas S. Salmier, October 8, 1862, ch. 6, vol. 641, pg. 13, Letters Sent, June 28, 1862–August 29, 1863, Medical Director's Office, Army of Northern Virginia, RG 109.
376. See Notes in regard to Confederate wounded (Supplies), Tayloe Family Papers, VHS. Such companionship was not always the case, however. For an instance of mistreatment of Confederate wounded by Union soldiers, see Forrest, *Old Soldier's Career*, second and third unpaginated leaves.
377. *OR* vol. 19, pt. 1, 112.

378. See Mitchell, "Recollections," *B&L*, 2:690, which mentions a few Confederate doctors who came to Shepherdstown following the Battle of South Mountain but also states, "With a few honorable exceptions—[they all] might as well have staid [*sic*] away." This is one of the only references Mitchell makes to the Confederate medical corps in Shepherdstown and speaks mainly of women and children taking care of their wounded guests.
379. See Thomas S. Waring to Rebecca Waring, October [2?], 1862, Thomas Waring Papers, South Caroliniana Library, University of South Carolina. Waring also mentions in a letter dated September 28, 1862, that by that date, "Nearly all of our Sick and wounded have been taken to Winchester."
380. Lafayette Guild to unknown, November 29, 1862, ch. 6, vol. 641, pg. 45, Letters Sent, June 28, 1862–August 29, 1863, Medical Director's Office, Army of Northern Virginia, RG 109; William A. Carswell Compiled Service Record, roll 0050, M 331, Compiled service records of Confederate officers and enlisted men who did not belong to any particular regiment, separate company or comparable unit, or special corps, RG 109.
381. Alexander Tinsley Biography, Tinsley Alumni File, W&M.
382. *Shepherdstown Register*, "Death Is Ever Busy," November 21, 1912.
383. Tinsley to Swem, February 6, 1939, Tinsley Alumni File, W&M; *Shepherdstown Register*, "Death Is Ever Busy."
384. Alexander Tinsley to Earl G. Swem, January 28, 1939, Tinsley Alumni File, W&M.
385. For an example of Union intentions to capture Confederate wounded in Shepherdstown, see Randolph B. Marcy to Fitz John Porter, September 22, 1862, 2:00 p.m., *OR* vol. 19, pt. 2, 344.
386. *New York Times*, "Reconnoisances [*sic*] Across the Potomac," October 1, 1862; *OR* vol. 19, pt. 2, 367.
387. Hard, *Eighth Cavalry*, 190.
388. *OR* vol. 19, pt. 2, 657.
389. Pritchard, *Colonel D. Wyatt Aiken*, 39; *Charleston (SC) Tri-Weekly Courier*, "From Our Army," September 30, 1862.
390. Dickert, *Kershaw's Brigade*, 164–65.
391. Betts, *Experience of a Confederate Chaplain*, 20.
392. *OR* vol. 19, pt. 1, 1,027.
393. Warfield, *Memoirs*, 102–03.
394. Wallace, *17th Virginia Infantry*, 116.
395. Tinsley to Swem, February 6, 1939, Tinsley Alumni File, W&M.

396. Civil War Service, Notes of Annie Cox Barlow, private collection; John H. Barlow Compiled Service Record, roll 0780, M 324, Compiled Service Records of Confederate Soldiers Who Served in Organizations from the State of Virginia, RG 109; Thomas J. Barlow Compiled Service Record, roll 0780, M 324, Compiled Service Records of Confederate Soldiers Who Served in Organizations from the State of Virginia, RG 109.
397. Civil War Service, Notes of Annie Cox Barlow, private collection.
398. Society of the Lees of Virginia, "Recollections of Netta Lee," 14.
399. Lee to Rust, October 3, 1862, Goldsborough Family Papers, Scarborough Library, Shepherd University.
400. Civil War Service, Notes of Annie Cox Barlow, private collection.
401. White, *31st Georgia Volunteer Infantry*, 54.
402. Sarah Page Andrews to unknown, September 22, 1862, CWA Papers.
403. Find a Grave, "Willoughby Farquhar Trezevant."
404. Sarah Page Andrews to Page Andrews, September 18, 1862, CWA Papers.
405. Lee to Rust, October 3, 1862, Goldsborough Family Papers, Scarborough Library, Shepherd University.
406. *New York Times*, "Pictures of the Dead at Antietam," 5.

Chapter 9

407. White, *Richmond Howitzer Battalion*, 195.
408. Nisbet, *Four Years*, 112.
409. *OR* vol. 19, pt. 2, 659–60.
410. John Francis Shaffner to Christian Thomas Pfohl, October 3, 1862, Christian Thomas Pfohl Papers, #3331, SHC.
411. See *OR* vol. 19, pt. 1, 878.
412. Gaillard, *Civil War Letters*, 24.
413. *OR* vol. 19, pt. 2, 621; *OR* vol. 19, pt. 2, 713. Of course, this growth in strength cannot alone be attributed to the medical corps mending wounded men. On October 18, 1862, Reverend James B. Sheeran of the Fourteenth Louisiana Infantry recorded in his diary, "I had not seen the army in such a good condition as this morning. The stragglers and those broken down were all up with their commands; besides many wounded had returned from the hospitals, recovered from their wounds." Sheeran, *Confederate Chaplain*, 33. The Army of Northern Virginia's strength grew from 41,520 on September 22 to 83,385 on November 11, 1862.

414. See Alexander, *Military Memoirs of a Confederate*, 223, for a description of the Confederate soldier at the onset of the Maryland Campaign.
415. Turner, *Civil War Letters*, 57.
416. Tribble, *Benjamin Cason Rawlings*, 61.
417. Pritchard, *Colonel D. Wyatt Aiken*, 39.
418. Netta Lee Cox notes, Notes of Annie Cox Barlow, private collection.
419. *Shepherdstown Register*, "A Reminder of the Battle of Antietam," June 6, 1918.
420. Hartzell, *On This Rock*, 62.
421. Robert Douglas to Fitz John Porter, October 24, 1862, M345, Union Provost Marshals' File of Paper Relating to Individual Civilians, roll 0076, RG 109.
422. Dr. John Quigley journal, Box 7, Shepherdstown, West Virginia, Papers, 1808–1945, accession #11104, Special Collections Dept., University of Virginia Library, Charlottesville, VA.
423. *See Shepherd's Town*, 3:117; Lee to Rust, October 3, 1862, Goldsborough Family Papers, Scarborough Library, Shepherd University.
424. *Shepherdstown Register*, "The Confederate Dead," August 25, 1865.
425. Ibid., "The Change of Time and the War," July 22, 1865, reprinted in *Shepherdstown Register*, December 4, 1949, Section C.
426. Frazier, "Monument at Shepherdstown," 113.
427. Stotelmyer, *Bivouacs of the Dead*, 55.
428. Frazier, "Monument at Shepherdstown," 113.
429. Stotelmyer, *Bivouacs of the Dead*, 55.
430. Frazier, "Monument at Shepherdstown," 113.
431. *See Shepherd's Town*, 3:118–21.
432. Mitchell, "Recollections," *B&L*, 2:695.

BIBLIOGRAPHY

Manuscripts

Andrews, Charles Wesley. Papers. David M. Rubenstein Rare Book and Manuscript Library, Duke University.

Atkinson, Archibald, Jr. Memoir. Virginia Polytechnic and State University, Special Collections, Blacksburg, VA.

Barlow, Annie Cox. Notes. Private Collection.

Boulware, James Richmond. Diary, 1862–1863. Library of Virginia.

Campbell Family Papers. Earl Gregg Swem Library, College of William and Mary.

Civil War Papers, 1862–1865. Robert Manning Strozier Library, Florida State University.

Clark, Thomas. Letters. State Archives of Florida, Florida Department of State.

Coleman, Clayton G. Papers. Virginia Military Institute Archives.

Fries and Shaffner Family Papers. Southern Historical Collection, University of North Carolina at Chapel Hill.

Gilpin, E.N. Papers. Manuscripts Division, Library of Congress.

Goldsborough Family Papers. Scarborough Library, Shepherd University.

Holloway, R.G. Diary. Fourth Texas Infantry. Eleanor S. Brockenbrough Archives, Museum of the Confederacy.

Hotchkiss, Jedediah. Papers. Manuscripts Division, Library of Congress.

John H. Nelson Collection. Antietam National Battlefield.

Lancaster, Robert Alexander. Papers. Virginia Historical Society.

Mary Bedinger Mitchell Biography. Historic Shepherdstown Museum.
Medical/Hospital Collection. Eleanor S. Brockenbrough Archives, Museum of the Confederacy.
Medical Personnel Collection. Eleanor S. Brockenbrough Archives, Museum of the Confederacy.
Parker, Francis M. Papers. Southern Historical Collection, University of North Carolina at Chapel Hill.
Pfohl, Christian Thomas. Papers. Southern Historical Collection, University of North Carolina at Chapel Hill.
Records of the Adjutant General's Office. Record Group 94. National Archives.
Rives Family Papers. Virginia Historical Society.
Shepherdstown, West Virginia Papers. University of Virginia Library.
Stuart, James Ewell Brown. Papers. Henry E. Huntington Library, San Marino, CA.
Tayloe Family Papers. Virginia Historical Society.
Thirteenth Georgia Volunteer Infantry Regiment File. Antietam National Battlefield.
Twenty-second North Carolina Folder. Gettysburg National Military Park.
University Archives. Faculty-Alumni File Collection. Earl Gregg Swem Library, College of William and Mary.
Waller, George E. Letters. Southern Historical Collection, University of North Carolina at Chapel Hill.
War Department Collection of Confederate Records. Record Group 109. National Archives.
Wardlaw, Andrew B. Diary. Antietam National Battlefield.
Waring, Thomas. Papers. South Caroliniana Library, University of South Carolina.
Weisiger, David Addison. Papers. Virginia Historical Society.

Newspapers

Atlanta Southern Confederacy
Charleston (SC) Mercury
Charleston (SC) Tri-Weekly Courier
(Charlestown) Virginia Free Press
Fayetteville (NC) Semi-Weekly Observer
Monroe (GA) Advertiser
New York Times

North Carolina Standard
Our Living and Our Dead (New Bern, NC)
Raleigh Spirit of the Age
Raleigh Weekly Standard
Richmond Daily Dispatch
Richmond Dispatch
Rockingham (Harrisonburg, VA) Register
Savannah (GA) Daily Morning News
Shepherdstown Register

Published Sources

Albert, Allen D., ed. *History of the Forty-Fifth Regiment Pennsylvania Veteran Volunteer Infantry, 1861–1865*. Williamsport, PA: Grit Publishing Company, 1912.

Alexander, Edward Porter. *Fighting for the Confederacy: The Personal Recollections of General Edward Porter Alexander*. Edited by Gary W. Gallagher. Chapel Hill: University of North Carolina Press, 1989.

———. *Military Memoirs of a Confederate: A Critical Narrative*. New York: Charles Scribner's Sons, 1907.

Andrews, William H. *Footprints of a Regiment: A Recollection of the 1st Georgia Regulars, 1861–1865*. Atlanta, GA: Longstreet Press, 1992.

Bartlett, Napier. *Military Record of Louisiana*. New Orleans: L. Graham & Co., 1875.

Battle, Cullen Andrews. *Third Alabama! The Civil War Memoir of Brigadier General Cullen Andrews Battle, CSA*. Edited by Brandon H. Beck. Tuscaloosa: University of Alabama Press, 2000.

Belfoure, Charles. "Historic Structures Report for the Mecklenburg Tobacco Warehouse." Friends of the Shepherdstown Riverfront. March 20, 2010. http://www.shepherdstownriverfront.org/wp-content/uploads/2012/06/MTWhsr.pdf (accessed April 15, 2015).

Benson, Berry. *Berry Benson's Civil War Book: Memoirs of a Confederate Scout and Sharpshooter*. Edited by Susan Williams Benson. Athens: University of Georgia Press, 1992.

Bernard, George S., ed. *War Talks of Confederate Veterans*. Petersburg, VA: Fenn & Owen, 1892.

Betts, A.D. *Experience of a Confederate Chaplain, 1861–1864*. Edited by W.A. Betts. N.p., 1900.

BIBLIOGRAPHY

Black, Harvey. *A Surgeon with Stonewall Jackson: The Civil War Letters of Dr. Harvey Black*. Edited by Glenn L. McMullen. Baltimore, MD: Butternut and Blue, 1995.

Blackford, Susan Leigh, and Charles Minor Blackford. *Letters from Lee's Army*. Lincoln: University of Nebraska Press, 1998.

Blanton, Wyndham B. *Medicine in Virginia in the Nineteenth Century*. Richmond, VA: Garrett & Massie, Incorporated, 1933.

Bradwell, Isaac Gordon. *Under the Southern Cross: Soldier Life with Gordon Bradwell and the Army of Northern Virginia*. Edited by Pharris Deloach Johnson. Macon, GA: Mercer University Press, 1999.

Caldwell, J.F.J. *The History of a Brigade of South Carolinians, Known First as "Gregg's," and Subsequently as "McGowan's Brigade."* Philadelphia: King & Baird, 1866.

Carman, Ezra A. *The Maryland Campaign of September 1862*. Edited by Thomas G. Clemens. Vol. 2. *Antietam*. El Dorado Hills, CA: Savas Beatie, 2012.

Chalmers, James R. "Lieutenant-General N.B. Forrest and His Campaigns." *Southern Historical Society Papers* 7 (October 1879): 451–86.

Cole, R.T. *From Huntsville to Appomattox: R.T. Coles's History of 4th Regiment, Alabama Volunteer Infantry, C.S.A., Army of Northern Virginia*. Edited by Jeffrey D. Stocker. Knoxville: University of Tennessee Press, 1996.

Conway, Martin R. *Shepherdstown: An American Treasure*. Shepherdstown, WV: Carabelle Books, 1991.

Cordell, Eugene Fauntleroy. *The Medical Annals of Maryland: 1799–1899*. Baltimore: Medical and Chirurgical Faculty of the State of Maryland, 1903.

Cunningham, Horace H. *Doctors in Gray: The Confederate Medical Service*. Baton Rouge: Louisiana State University Press, 1986.

———. *Field Medical Services at the Battles of Manassas (Bull Run)*. Athens: University of Georgia Press, 1968.

Cutts, Allen S. "A.S. Cutts to Dr. J. William Jones." *Southern Historical Society Papers* 10, nos. 1–2 (January–February 1882): 429–31.

Denney, Robert E. *Civil War Medicine: Care & Comfort of the Wounded*. New York: Sterling Publishing Co., Inc., 1994.

DeRosset, William L. "Additional Sketch Third Regiment." In *Histories of the Several Regiments and Battalions from North Carolina in the Great War 1861–'65*. Edited by Walter Clark. Vol. 1. Raleigh, NC: R.M. Uzzell, 1901, 226.

Dickert, D. Augustus. *History of Kershaw's Brigade*. Newberry, SC: Elbert H. Aull Company, 1899.

Dinkins, James. *1861 to 1865, by an Old Johnie: Personal Recollections and Experiences in the Confederate Army*. Cincinnati, OH: Robert Clarke Co., 1897.

BIBLIOGRAPHY

Dooley, John E. *John Dooley, Confederate Soldier: His War Journal*. Edited by Joseph T. Durkin. Washington, D.C.: Georgetown University Press, 1945.

Douglas, Henry Kyd. *I Rode with Stonewall*. Chapel Hill: University of North Carolina Press, 1968.

Duncan, Louis C. *The Medical Department of the United States Army in the Civil War*. N.p.: Louis C. Duncan, n.d.

Eicher, John H., and David J. Eicher. *Civil War High Commands*. Stanford, CA: Stanford University Press, 2001.

Farr, Warner Dahlgren. "Samuel Preston Moore: Confederate Surgeon General." *Civil War History* 41, no. 1 (March 1995): 41–56.

Find a Grave. "Willoughby Farquhar Trezevant (1846–1862)—Find a Grave Memorial." September 29, 2011. http://www.findagrave.com/cgi-bin/fg.cgi?page=gr&GSln=trezevant&GSbyrel=all&GSdy=1862&GSdyrel=in&GSob=n&GRid=77255350&df=all& (accessed April 29, 2015).

Forrest, T. Frank. *An Old Soldier's Career: His Four Long Years Experience, Trials, and Sufferings in the Bloody Conflict of the Sixties*. Stewart, MS: n.p., 1906.

Frazier, J.W.B. "Monument at Shepherdstown, W. Va." *Confederate Veteran*, March 1902.

Freemon, Frank R. *Gangrene and Glory: Medical Care during the American Civil War*. Urbana: University of Illinois Press, 2001.

Gaillard, Fred E., ed. *Franklin Gaillard's Civil War Letters*. n.p., 1969.

Gentile, Mannie. "Hidden, in Plain Sight: Terrain at Antietam." Antietam Journal (blog), January 1, 2013. http://antietamjournal.blogspot.com/2013/02/hidden-in-plain-sight-terrain-at.html (accessed March 18, 2015).

Haller, John S., Jr. *Battlefield Medicine: A History of the Military Ambulance from the Napoleonic Wars through World War I*. Carbondale: Southern Illinois University Press, 2011.

Hard, Abner. *History of the Eighth Cavalry Regiment Illinois Volunteers, During the Great Rebellion*. Aurora, IL: n.p., 1868.

Harsh, Joseph L. *Sounding the Shallows: A Confederate Companion for the Maryland Campaign of 1862*. Kent, OH: Kent State University Press, 2000.

———. *Taken at the Flood: Robert E. Lee & Confederate Strategy in the Maryland Campaign of 1862*. Kent, OH: Kent State University Press, 1999.

Hartwig, D. Scott. *To Antietam Creek: The Maryland Campaign of September 1862*. Baltimore, MD: Johns Hopkins University Press, 2012.

Hartzell, Gladys. *On This Rock: The Story of St. Peter's Church, Shepherdstown, 1765–1965*. Shepherdstown, WV: Shepherdstown Register, 1970.

Hewett, Janet B., Noah Andre Trudeau and Bryce A. Suderow, eds. *Supplement to the Official Records of the Union and Confederate Armies*. Vol. 3. Wilmington, NC: Broadfoot Publishing Company, 1994.

Holsworth, Jerry W. "Uncommon Valor: Hood's Texas Brigade in the Maryland Campaign." *Blue and Gray Magazine*, August 1996.

Hood, John B. *Advance and Retreat: Personal Experiences in the United States and Confederate States Armies*. New Orleans: G.T. Beauregard, 1880.

Hoptak, John David. *The Battle of South Mountain*. Charleston, SC: The History Press, 2011.

Hotchkiss, Jedediah. *Make Me a Map of the Valley: The Civil War Journal of Stonewall Jackson's Topographer*. Edited by Archie P. McDonald. Dallas, TX: Southern Methodist University Press, 1973.

Hubbs, G. Ward, ed. *Voices from Company D: Diaries by the Greensboro Guards, Fifth Alabama Infantry Regiment, Army of Northern Virginia*. Athens: University of Georgia Press, 2003.

Hunter, Alexander. *Johnny Reb and Billy Yank*. New York: Neale Publishing Company, 1905.

Jensen, Les. *32nd Virginia Infantry*. Lynchburg, VA: H.E. Howard, Inc., 1990.

Johnson, Robert Underwood, and Clarence Clough Buel. *Battles and Leaders of the Civil War.* Vol. 2. New York: Century Co., 1884–1887.

Jordan, Weymouth T., Jr., and Louis H. Manarin. *North Carolina Troops, 1861–1865: A Roster*. Vol. 6, *Infantry: 16th–18th and 20th–21st Regiments*. Raleigh: North Carolina Division of Archives and History, 1977.

Kenamond, A.D. *Prominent Men of Shepherdstown During Its First 200 Years*. Charles Town, WV: Jefferson County Historical Society, 1963.

Krick, Robert K. *Lee's Colonels: A Biographical Register of the Field Officers of the Army of Northern Virginia*. 4th ed. Dayton, OH: Morningside House, Inc., 1992.

Lee, Edmund Jennings. *Lee of Virginia, 1642–1892: Biographical and Genealogical Sketches of the Descendants of Colonel Richard Lee*. Philadelphia, PA: Edmund Jennings Lee, 1895.

Lee, Laura Elizabeth. *Forget-Me-Nots of the Civil War: A Romance, Containing Reminiscences and Original Letters of Two Confederate Soldiers*. St. Louis, MO: A.R. Fleming Printing, 1909.

Lee, Mary Greenhow. *The Civil War Journal of Mary Greenhow Lee (Mrs. Hugh Holmes Lee) of Winchester, Virginia*. Edited by Eloise C. Strader. Winchester, VA: Winchester-Frederick County Historical Society, 2011.

Lee, Susan P. *Memoirs of William Nelson Pendleton, D.D.* Harrisonburg, VA: Sprinkle Publications, 1991.

Luvaas, Jay, and Harold W. Nelson, eds. *The U.S. Army War College Guide to the Battle of Antietam, the Maryland Campaign of 1862*. Carlisle, PA: South Mountain Press, Inc., Publishers, 1987.

Mason, Emily V. *Popular Life of Gen. Robert Edward Lee*. Baltimore, MD: John Murphy & Co., 1874.

McClellan, Henry B. *I Rode with Jeb Stuart: The Life and Campaigns of Major General J.E.B. Stuart*. Edited by Burke Davis. Boston: Da Capo Press, 1994.

McDaniel, J.J. *Diary of Battles, Marches, and Incidents of the Seventh S.C. Regiment*. N.p., 1862.

Meier, Kathryn S. "'No Place for the Sick': Nature's War on Civil War Soldier Mental and Physical Health in the 1862 Peninsula and Shenandoah Valley Campaigns." *Journal of the Civil War Era* 1, no. 2 (June 2011): 176–206.

Monroe, J. Albert. *Battery D, First Rhode Island Light Artillery, at the Battle of Antietam, September 17, 1862*. Providence: Rhode Island Soldiers and Sailors Historical Society, 1886.

Moore, Edward A. *The Story of a Cannoneer Under Stonewall Jackson*. New York: Neale Publishing Company, 1907.

Musser, Clifford S. *Two Hundred Years' History of Shepherdstown*. Shepherdstown, WV: The Independent, 1931.

National Park Service: Antietam National Battlefield. "Antietam: People and Places." http://www.nps.gov/anti/learn/education/upload/People-and-Places.pdf (accessed March 30, 2015).

Neese, George M. *Three Years in the Confederate Horse Artillery*. New York: Neale Publishing Company, 1911.

Nisbet, James Cooper. *Four Years on the Firing Line*. Edited by Bell Irvin Wiley. Jackson, TN: McCowat-Mercer Press, Inc., 1963.

Owen, William. *In Camp and Battle with the Washington Artillery of New Orleans*. Boston: Ticknor and Company, 1885.

Pritchard, Claudius Hornby, Jr. *Colonel D. Wyatt Aiken, 1828–1887: South Carolina's Militant Agrarian*. Hampden-Sydney, VA: Claudius Hornby Pritchard Jr., 1970.

Rafuse, Ethan S. *A Single Grand Victory: The First Campaign and Battle of Manassas*. Wilmington, DE: Scholarly Resources Inc., 2002.

Reese, Timothy J. *Sealed with Their Lives: The Battle for Crampton's Gap, Burkittsville, Maryland, September 14, 1862*. Baltimore, MD: Butternut & Blue, 1998.

Reilly, O.T. *The Battlefield of Antietam*. Sharpsburg, MD: Oliver T. Reilly, 1906.

Scott, W.W. *A History of Orange County Virginia*. Richmond, VA: Everett Waddey Co., 1907.

Sears, Stephen W. *To the Gates of Richmond: The Peninsula Campaign*. New York: Ticknor & Fields, 1992.

See Shepherd's Town. Vol. 3. Shepherdstown, WV: Historic Shepherdstown Commission, 1997.

Shaw, Maurice F. *Stonewall Jackson's Surgeon: Hunter Holmes McGuire, A Biography*. Lynchburg, VA: H.E. Howard, Inc., 1993.

Sheeran, James B. *Confederate Chaplain: A War Journal of Rev. James B. Sheeran, c.ss.r 14th Louisiana, C.S.A.* Edited by Joseph T. Durkin. Milwaukee, WI: Bruce Publishing Company, 1969.

Shotwell, Randolph Abbott. *The Papers of Randolph Abbott Shotwell*. Edited by J.G. de Roulhac Hamilton and Rebecca Cameron. Vol. 1. Raleigh: North Carolina Historical Commission, 1929.

Signature House Auction Catalog. November 30, 1996. Monkton, MD.

Silverman, Jason H., Samuel N. Thomas Jr. and Beverly D. Evans IV. *Shanks: The Life and Wars of General Nathan George Evans, C.S.A.* Cambridge, MA: Da Capo Press, 2002.

Snyder, Harry Lambright, III. *John Snyder 1823–1864: A Soldier and His Family*. Shepherdstown, WV: H.L. Snyder, 1999.

Society of the Lees of Virginia. "The Recollections of Netta Lee, 1861–1865." *Magazine of the Society of the Lees of Virginia* 6, nos. 1–2 (1928): 1–74.

Sorrel, G. Moxley. *Recollections of a Confederate Staff Officer*. New York: Neale Publishing Company, 1905.

Steiner, Lewis H. *Report of Lewis H. Steiner, M.D., Inspector of the Sanitary Commission, Containing a Diary kept during the Rebel Occupation of Frederick, Md. and an Account of the Operations of the U.S. Sanitary Commission During the Campaign in Maryland, September, 1862*. New York: Anson D.F. Randolph, 1862.

Stilwell, William R. *The Stilwell Letters: A Georgian in Longstreet's Corps, Army of Northern Virginia*. Edited by Ronald H. Moseley. Macon, GA: Mercer University Press, 2002.

Stone, DeWitt Boyd, ed. *Wandering to Glory: Confederate Veterans Remember Evans' Brigade*. Columbia: University of South Carolina Press, 2002.

Stotelmyer, Steven R. *The Bivouacs of the Dead*. Baltimore, MD: Toomey Press, 1992.

Stubbs, Steven H. *Duty, Honor, Valor: The Story of the Eleventh Mississippi Infantry Regiment*. Philadelphia, MS: Dancing Rabbit Press, Inc., 2000.

Sturkey, O. Lee. *Hampton Legion Infantry C.S.A.* Wilmington, NC: Broadfoot Publishing Company, 2008.

BIBLIOGRAPHY

Taylor, Walter Herron. *Lee's Adjutant: The Wartime Letters of Colonel Walter Herron Taylor, 1862–1865*. Edited by R. Lockwood Tower and John S. Belmont. Columbia: University of South Carolina Press, 1995.

Taylor, William H. *De Quibus*. Richmond, VA: Bell Book and Stationery Company, 1908.

Thomas, Emory M. *Robert E. Lee: A Biography*. New York: W.W. Norton & Company, 1997.

Thomas, Henry W. *History of the Doles-Cook Brigade, Army of Northern Virginia, C.S.A.* Atlanta, GA: Franklin Printing and Publishing Company, 1903.

Todd, George T. *First Texas Regiment*. Edited by Harold B. Simpson. Waco, TX: Texian Press, 1963.

Tribble, Byrd Barnette. *Benjamin Cason Rawlings: First Virginia Volunteer for the South*. Baltimore, MD: Butternut and Blue, 1995.

Trimpi, Helen. "Lafayette McLaws' Aide-de-Camp: The Maryland Campaign Diary of Captain Henry Lord Page King." *Civil War Regiments: A Journal of the American Civil War* 6, no. 2 (1998): 23–57.

Turner, Charles W., ed. *Civil War Letters of Arabella Speairs and William Beverley Pettit of Fluvanna County, Virginia March 1862–March 1865*. Vol. 1, *March 1862–February 1864*. Roanoke: Virginia Lithography & Graphics Company, 1988.

U.S. War Department. *The War of the Rebellion: A Compilation of the Official Records of the Union and Confederate Armies*. 128 vols. Washington, D.C.: GPO, 1880–1901.

Virginia Memory. "Map of April 17, 1861, Vote On Secession." 2014. http://www.virginiamemory.com/docs/hires/april_17_1861_vote.pdf (accessed January 27, 2015).

Virginia Military Institute. "VMI Historical Archives Rosters: William Sellman Parran." http://archivesweb.vmi.edu/rosters/record.php?ID=516 (accessed April 5, 2015).

Von Borcke, Heros. *Memoirs of the Confederate War for Independence*. Vol. 1. Edinburgh: William Blackwood and Sons, 1866.

Walker, Charles D. *Biographical Sketches of the Graduates and Élèves of the Virginia Military Institute Who Fell During the War Between the States*. Philadelphia, PA: J.B. Lippincott & Co., 1875.

Walker, Cornelius. *Memoir of Rev. C.W. Andrews, D.D.* New York: Thomas Whittaker, 1877.

Wallace, Lee A. Jr. *17th Virginia Infantry*. Lynchburg, VA: H.E. Howard, Inc., 1990.

Warfield, Edgar. *Manassas to Appomattox: The Civil War Memoirs of Pvt. Edgar Warfield, 17th Virginia Infantry*. McLean, VA: EPM Publications, Inc., 1996.

BIBLIOGRAPHY

Waters, Zack C., and James C. Edmonds. *A Small but Spartan Band: The Florida Brigade in Lee's Army of Northern Virginia*. Tuscaloosa: University of Alabama Press, 2010.

Weaver, Jeffrey C., and Lee A. Wallace Jr. *Richmond Ambulance Co., Herbig's Infirmary Co. and The Virginia Public Guard and Armory Band*. Lynchburg, VA: H.E. Howard, Inc., 1985.

Welch, Spencer Glasgow. *A Confederate Surgeon's Letters to His Wife*. New York: Neale Publishing Company, 1911.

Welch, Stephen Elliott. *Stephen Elliott Welch of the Hampton Legion*. Edited by John Michael Priest. Vol. 3. Civil War Heritage Series. Shippensburg, PA: Burd Street Press, 1994.

White, Gregory C. *A History of the 31st Georgia Volunteer Infantry: Lawton-Gordon-Evans Brigade, Army of Northern Virginia, Confederate States of America, 1861–1865*. Baltimore, MD: Butternut and Blue, 1997.

White, William S. *Contributions to a History of the Richmond Howitzer Battalion*. Vol. 2, *A Diary of the War, or What I Saw of It*. Richmond, VA: Carlton McCarthy & Co., 1883.

Wise, George. *History of the Seventeenth Virginia Infantry, C.S.A.* Baltimore, MD: Kelly, Piet & Company, 1870.

Zax, David. "Civil War Geology." Smithsonian. April 13, 2009. http://www.smithsonianmag.com/history/civil-war-geology-123489220/?no-ist=&page=1 (accessed March 18, 2015).

INDEX

A

Aiken, D. Wyatt 41, 78, 79, 93, 121, 129, 130
Alabama, Fourth Infantry 42, 50
Alabama, Third Infantry 43
ambulance corps. *See* Confederate medical corps
Anderson, George B. 80, 81, 82, 88, 103, 104
Andrews, Charles 30, 34, 62, 69, 100
Andrews, Sarah Page 93, 100, 125
army medical boards 19, 26, 63
Atwell, James B. 42, 77, 114

B

Barlow, John "Jack" 79, 80, 98, 122, 130
Barlow, Thomas 79, 98, 122, 124
Baruch, Simon 43, 44, 54, 55, 142
Bedford 80, 98, 102, 122, 124
Bernard, George 45, 46
Boonsboro, Maryland 53, 54, 55, 57, 58
Boteler, Margie 103
Boteler's Ford 27, 49, 58, 59, 63, 93, 94, 109, 111, 112
Brown, John 30, 100

C

Carswell, William A. 118
Clark, Thomas 66, 82, 113
Confederate medical corps. *See* Confederate medical department
Confederate medical department 18, 19, 20, 22, 26, 38, 41, 42, 47, 52, 75, 85, 118, 127, 128, 129
Cook, Henry A. 124, 125
Crampton's Gap 39, 46, 52, 57
Crowder, John T. 72

D

DeLeon, David C. 20
DeRosset, William L. 76, 77, 121, 122
Douglas Hill 101
Douglas, Robert 130
Douglass, Marcellus 71, 72

E

Elmwood Cemetery 130, 131, 132
Evans, Nathan 25, 83

INDEX

F

Ferry Hill Place 56, 65, 73, 130
First Manassas, Battle of 18, 52
Florida, Eighth Infantry 81, 82
Florida, Fifth Infantry 81, 82
Fox's Gap 39, 42, 57
Frederick, Maryland 13, 36, 37, 38, 39, 139

G

Gaines, John Mutius 54, 55
General Orders No. 94 22, 128
Gorman, John 42, 81, 82
Grove farm 86, 93
Guild, Lafayette 20, 21, 22, 24, 25, 26, 37, 53, 54, 57, 58, 65, 86, 87, 106, 115, 117, 118, 128

H

Hall, William J. 85, 122
Hampton Legion 73, 74, 130
Harpers Ferry, (West) Virginia 30, 39, 41, 57, 120, 133
Heard, John 53
Herbig, John 53
Herbig's infirmary corps 53, 65
Herndon, James 25, 65
Hood, John Bell 25, 42
Hoyt, John 43

I

infirmary corps. *See* Confederate medical department

J

Jefferson County, (West) Virginia 28, 30

L

Lawton, Alexander 72, 98
Lee, Henrietta Bedinger 123, 125, 131
Lee, Henrietta "Netta" 33, 61, 98, 124, 130
Lee, Robert E. 20, 22, 24, 25, 37, 39, 44, 52, 53, 67, 86, 87, 94, 97, 106, 111, 120, 128, 140
Lee, W.H.F. "Rooney" 55, 56, 98
Letterman, Jonathan 22, 94, 117
Liddell, Phillip Franklin 65, 100

M

Maryland Heights 39, 41, 47, 57
McLemore, Owen K. 42, 43
Mississippi, Eleventh Infantry 65
Mitchell, Mary Bedinger 31, 32, 34, 49, 61, 62, 63, 64, 76, 91, 102, 133
Moore, Samuel Preston 18, 19
Moulder Hall 92
Mt. Airy. *See* Grove farm

N

North Carolina, Second Infantry 42
North Carolina, Third Infantry 76

P

Parran family 32, 33, 61, 76, 84, 106, 118
Parran, William Sellman 33, 84, 106, 138
Pendleton, William Nelson 111
Piper farm 81, 82, 88
Pleasant Valley 47, 57
Pleasonton, Alfred 109, 151
Porter, Fitz John 109, 111

Q

Quigley, John 63, 92, 130, 131
Quigley, Julia 131

R

Reel farm 79, 89
Rentch, Daniel 77, 114
Richmond, Virginia 19, 20, 36, 93
Rickard, Elijah 100

INDEX

S

Second Manassas, Battle of 23, 37, 38, 52
Seven Pines, Battle of 20
Sharpsburg, Maryland 13, 35, 57, 59, 63, 64, 75, 76, 83, 115
Shenandoah Valley 27, 36, 39, 104, 105, 132
Shotwell, Randolph Abbott 51, 101
Smith, Henry Julius 73, 74, 130
Sorrel, Moxley 49
South Carolina, Fourteenth Infantry 111, 113
South Carolina, Seventh Infantry 78
Staunton, Virginia 36, 93, 104, 120

T

Tinsley, Alexander 118, 120, 122
Todd, George 74
Trezevant, Willoughby Farquhar 83, 100, 125, 161
Trinity Episcopal Church 30, 98
Turner's Gap 39

V

Virginia, Seventeenth Infantry 84, 85
Virginia, Thirty-second Infantry 79

W

Warfield, Edgar 85, 96, 122
Welch, Stephen Elliott 74
Williamsburg, Battle of 19
Willis, Robert T. 80, 98, 123
Winchester, Virginia 33, 36, 37, 43, 65, 93, 97, 103, 105, 106
Wingfield, Thomas H. 37
Wise Artillery 84
Wright, Bird 82, 114

Y

Young, William Proby 77

ABOUT THE AUTHOR

Kevin Pawlak is a Civil War historian who works as a licensed battlefield guide at Antietam National Battlefield and as an education specialist for the Mosby Heritage Area Association. Previously, he has worked and completed internships at Harpers Ferry National Historical Park, the Papers of Abraham Lincoln at the Abraham Lincoln Presidential Library and the Missouri Civil War Museum. Kevin graduated in 2014 from Shepherd University, where he studied Civil War history and historic preservation. When he is not studying the Civil War, Kevin runs marathons.

The author at the local Civil War monument in his hometown of Albion, New York. *Courtesy of Jerome Pawlak.*